Basic Guide
for
Enterprise Linux®
Servers

Basic Guide
for
Enterprise Linux®
Servers

Mihail Buzarin

To order additional copies of this book, contact:
Xlibris Corporation
1-888-795-4274
www.Xlibris.com
Orders@Xlibris.com
74664

Contents

Introduction 9

Chapter 1. Installation 11

Chapter 2. Configuring partitions 25

Chapter 3. Managing users, groups and permissions in Linux® 49

Chapter 4. Package management 78

Chapter 5. Basic system configuration tools 86

Chapter 6. The Web Server Package Group: Apache and Squid 114

Chapter 7. Sharing Files On Network: NFS, FTP, Samba 139

Chapter 8: Mail Server 161

Chapter 9. SSH, NTP and XINETD 175

Chapter 10. Domain Name Service – DNS 187

Chapter 11. DHCP – Dynamic Host Configuration Protocol 204

Chapter 12. Network Information System (NIS) 217

Chapter 13. Securing Access To Services 228

Chapter 14. Using Firewall and SELinux 247

Hats off to Linux® developers
famous or anonymous from allover the world.

To all my family and friends
from both sides of the ocean.

Introduction

This book might be a good help for anyone who wants to understand and practice the basic configuration of different servers using Red Hat® Enterprise Linux® based distributions.
In this case the best Linux® distributions for practicing are CentOS available for download at **http://mirror.centos.org/**and Scientific Linux available at **https://www.scientificlinux.org/download.**

Both distributions will serve you very good once installed on Desktops.
These distributions were rebuilt using the released source code of Red Hat® Enterprise Linux® and they will be very useful for practicing especially if in the future you will want to prepare for the Red Hat Certified Engineer (RHCE™) exam.

If you want to practice on a Laptop be sure first to consult your Laptop Manufacturer's website.
Search the support section to be sure that the Linux® distribution you want to download will work on your Laptop.

After you downloaded and installed one of the above Linux® distributions I also recommend to use **Vmware-server-[version_number].rpm** available for download at **http://www.vmware.com/.**

This way your day by day operating system won't suffer any modification but providing only the support for virtual machines you'll want to practice with.

In case your daily operating system is a Microsoft® product, the VMware Team offers you **Vmware-server-[version_number].exe**.

What follows describes briefly the installation of a Linux® based Virtual Machine.
Supposing that you have already installed CentOS or Scientific Linux into your computer, in order to install and configure your **Vmware-server** be sure that you have installed the **xinetd-[version_number].rpm** package

*To verify the existence of the **xinetd-[version_number].rpm** package in your computer type from a terminal:*

> ***su -***
> ***rpm -qa | grep xinetd***

If the command returns no answer then you have to install this package. If you have an active Internet connection type from a terminal:

> ***su -***
> ***yum install xinetd***

If you don't have an active Internet connection then you can install the package from your installation DVD as follows:

- Open a terminal and become superuser:
  su -

- *If your CD-Rom or DVD-Rom is not already mounted let's mount it in the **/media** directory with the following command:*

  mount /dev/cdrom /media

- *Change directory into the directory that contains the rpm packages on your installation DVD and install the **xinetd** package:*

  cd /media/[directory_with_rpm_packages]/
  rpm -ivh xinetd-[version_number]

Note that some dependencies might be required !

- *After **xinetd-[version_number].rpm** package is installed proceed with the installation of the **Vmware-server-[version_number].rpm** package:*

  rpm -ivh Vmware-server-[version_number].rpm

Chapter 1.   Installation

As this book addresses to users familiar with Linux, I will not insist on installing CentOS or Scientific Linux using the set of installation CD's or DVD but I will present other installation methods.
I remind you that the best way to practice is using virtual machines so you will not damage your day by day operating system.

NFS (Network File System) Installation Server

Assuming that you have downloaded the installation DVD containing CentOS in order to configure a NFS Installation Server you have to follow these steps:

- First let's make a directory named **/install.** From this directory you will "serve" the necessary files over network:

  mkdir /install

- If **/dev/cdrom** is not mounted yet in **/media**, you have to mount it issuing this command from the terminal:

  mount /dev/cdrom /media

- Now that the CD/DVD-Rom is mounted in **/media** you have to copy the CentOS installation DVD into this folder:

  cp -ar /media/CentOS_dvd/. /install

In the expression above note the dot [.] at the end of **/media/** ! The dot says that the hidden files will be also copied. So don't forget the dot !!

- The **/install** directory needs to be properly exported. For this you
  need to open and edit the **/etc/exports** file with your favorite text
  editor and add the following line:

```
/install              *(ro,sync)
```

- After saving the changes in **/etc/exports** type:

exportfs -a

The command will export the directory **/install** over the network as read-only.
If you want to export this directory only for your LAN (Local Area Network)
and assuming that your computers in your LAN are part of a subnetwork with
the IP address 192.192.192.0 and netmask 255.255.255.0 the modification in
/etc/exports would look like this :

```
/install              192.192.192.0/255.255.255.0(ro,sync)
```

Note there are no spaces between characters in the
`192.192.192.0/255.255.255.0(ro,sync)` expression.

You'll have to replace the IP used in my example with yours.

- Make sure the Firewall is not blocking the access to the shared
  directory. For this you have to flush all iptables rules issuing the
  iptables -F command, or to disable Firewal with one of the **system-
  config-securitylevel** or, **system-config-securitylevel-tui** commands.

- If SELinux is activated (permissive or enforced mode) you have to
  disable it by using either the **system-config-securitylevel** command
  or **system-config-securitylevel-tui** command.

- Start the NFS service and make it functional also after rebooting the
  computer.

  service nfs status   - checks the status of the service (running or
  stopped)

  service nfs restart   - will restart the NFS service if already
  running

  chkconfig nfs on   - will start the service after an eventual
  computer reboot

Observations

*In real life **you will not stop** Firewall and SELinux because the security point of view matters !*
Other methods of keeping Firewall and SELinux running and accepting connections to your computer will be described later in this book.

If the NFS service is not starting then check if you have installed the **portmap-[version_number].rpm** package and the service **portmap** is running:

>   **rpm -qa | grep portmap**
>   **service portmap status**

Both daemons **nfs** and **portmap** must run in order to have a functional NFS server. The content of the **/etc/exports** file is seen by typing from a terminal:

>   **showmount -e**

If everything was configured correctly, your NFS server is ready to share the **/install** directory.

I assumed that this NFS server was installed on a virtual machine.
Now it's time to prepare a second virtual machine (let's name it NFS client) and make it ready to receive an operating system via NFS.

You need to create first a boot CD or a boot USB key.

To create a boot USB key:

- Insert your installation DVD or the first installation CD into the CD/DVD device.
- Plug-in your USB key
  To see where your USB key is mounted type from terminal:

>   **fdisk -l** and **mount -l**

- If the system will mount the CD/DVD device and the USB key in **/media**, then from a terminal type the following command:

>   **cat /media/CentOS_dvd/images/diskboot.img > /media/disk/diskboot.img**

Make sure that your USB key contains only the new created **diskboot.img** file.

To create a boot CD :

- Insert your installation DVD or the first installation CD into the CD/DVD device.
- From a terminal type:

  cp /media/CentOs_dvd/images/boot.iso /tmp

- After the file was copied eject your installation media and insert a blank CD into the CD/DVD device then type:

  cdrecord -v /tmp/boot.iso

Observations

You can create the boot USB key or the boot CD using the tools provided by the GUI interface of your preferred desktop manager (GNOME or KDM) but I suggest to use as much as possible the commands from the terminal.
Of course, it's easier apparently to use the tools provided by GNOME or KDE interface but doing this it's a time consuming job.

The purpose of creating a boot CD and/or boot USB key is to demonstrate the flexibility of Linux® installation when you don't have a handy installation CD/DVD but you have access to a shared directory (in our case /install) that shares the necessary files via NSF, FTP or, HTTP.
Also you can install your Linux® operating system if you've saved the content of the downloaded installation kit somewhere on your hard drive.
I will present all this methods in this chapter too.

- Insert the boot CD or plug-in the boot USB key you've just created into the NFS client computer and start or restart it making sure that you have establish the proper boot sequence in BIOS (boot from CD/DVD or, if BIOS allows, boot from USB).

- The **boot:** prompt will appear waiting for your command. Type:

linux askmethod

- You have to select a language for the installation process.

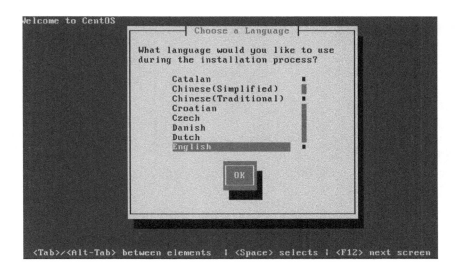

- Then you'll be prompted to select the type of keyboard.

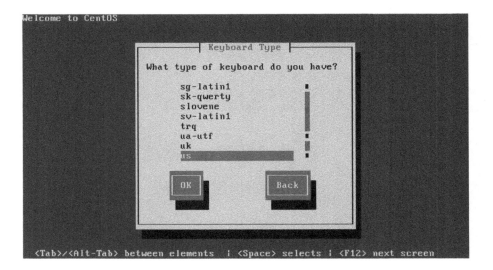

- Then you have to select what type of media contains the packages to be install. In this case you will select **NFS image.**

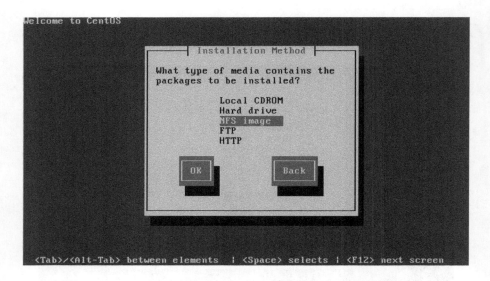

- In the next screen you'll be prompted to configure your TCP/IP settings.

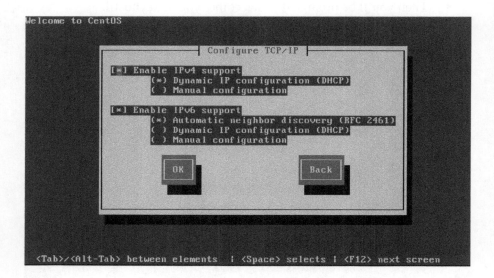

- Then you'll be asked to introduce some information regarding the NFS server's IP and the shared directory on this server.

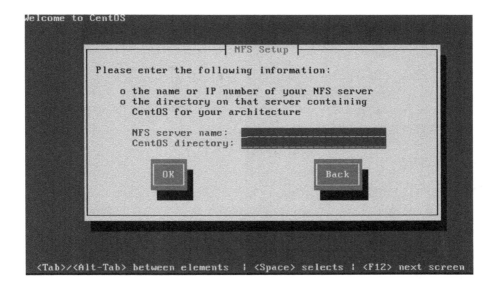

At this point you should know the IP address of the NFS server you have prepared. If not, from a terminal of your NFS server type :

>   **su -** (to become superuser)
>   **ifconfig eth0**

If you have an active Internet connection and the network settings are acquired through a DHCP server you will receive a set of information regarding the hardware of the machine you have prepared to be a NFS server, the IP address (**inet addr**), broadcast address (**Bcast:**) and mask (**Mask:**).

- I will use as an example the 192.192.192.1 IP address so in **NFS server name** type **192.192.192.1** and in **CentOS directory** type **/install.**

If the **/install** directory is exported properly and Firewall and SELinux are disabled (for the purpose of the exercise), when you select **OK** in the last screen, the CentOS installation should start with the Graphical User Interface.

FTP (File Transfer Protocol) installation server

Let's set up first a FTP server.

- Check the existence of the **vsftpd-[version_number].rpm** package on the computer that will be FTP server:

  rpm -qa | grep vsftpd

- If the package is not installed you can install it buy using **pirut** or by typing from a terminal :

  yum install vsftpd

You will need superuser rights (**su -**) for installing or upgrading any packages so you'll be prompted to introduce the superuser password no matter what method you'll use for installing.

After this package is installed I remind you that FTP server uses by default the **/var/ftp/pub** directory to serve shared files. In this directory you'll create the **/install** directory where you'll copy the content of the installation CD/DVD.

  mkdir /var/ftp/pub/install
  cp -ar /media/. /var/ftp/pub/install
Again, don't forget the dot [.] at the end of **/media** directory. It will copy all files including the hidden ones!

- Make sure to disable Firewall and SELinux so nothing will stand between your FTP server and FTP client. Not recommended but for now proceed like that.

- Start the FTP server and make it start also next time when you reboot the computer by issuing the following commands:

  service vsftpd start and eventually **chkconfig vsftpd on**

Observation
The default settings in the configuration file for the FTP server will share your /var/ftp/pub/install directory properly so you won't have to modify anything in the aforementioned file.
Use the cat /etc/vsftpd/vsftpd.conf | less command to read this file.

- On the computer that will be the client for your FTP server you'll follow the same steps as for the NFS client with the difference that now you have created already the boot CD or boot USB key and this time you have to select FTP as Installation Method.

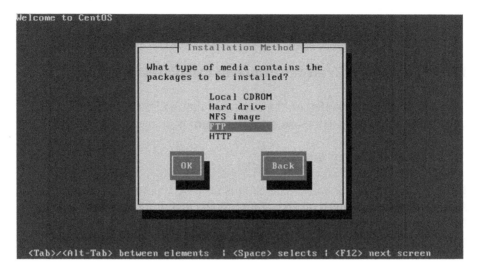

- In the next screen you have to introduce some information about the FTP server and the shared directory **/install**

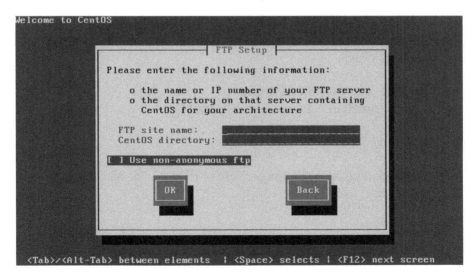

- For the field **FTP site name** type the IP address of your server determined as I've shown in the NFS server example.
- For the field **CentOS directory** type **/pub/install**

If everything is setup correctly in the next screen the CentOS installation should start with a Graphical User Interface.

HTTP (Hypertext Transfer Protocol) installation server

Check if you have installed on the computer that will be HTTP server the existence of the **httpd-[version_number].rpm** package:

rpm -qa | grep httpd

If the package is not installed you can install it by typing from a terminal **system-config-packages** or **pirut** (commands that will open the Package Manager tool if you want to use a graphical user interface) or simply just type :

yum install httpd

Again, I remind you that you'll need superuser rights (**su -**) for installing or upgrading any packages.
After this package is installed note that HTTP server uses by default the **/var/www/html** directory to serve shared files. In this directory you'll create the **/install** directory where you'll copy the installation CD/DVD of your operating system.

mkdir /var/www/html/install
cp -ar /media/. /var/www/html/install

Don't forget the dot [.] !

- Be sure to disable (for the purpose of the exercise only) Firewall and SELinux.

- Before starting the **httpd** service you have to disable the **welcome. conf** file of the server. This means that you'll have to comment out all the lines in this file by introducing in front of each one the pound (#) character.

  Open with a text editor the **/etc/httpd/conf.d/welcome.conf** file and make it look like this:

```
# This configuration file enables the default "Welcome"
# page if there is no default index page present for
# the root URL. To disable the Welcome page, comment
# out all the lines below.
#
#<LocationMatch "^/+$">
#    Options -Indexes
#    ErrorDocument 403 /error/noindex.html
#</LocationMatch>
```

- Start the **httpd** service and be sure it will start in case of a server reboot:

  service httpd start and **chkconfig httpd on**

Observation
The default configuration file of the httpd service will help you share properly your /var/www/html/install directory without modifying the aforementioned file.
Use the cat /etc/httpd/conf/httpd.conf command to view the file.
As for the client computer, the steps are similar with configuring a FTP client only that you have to choose HTTP as Installation Method and the next screen will ask you to provide information about the HTTP server's IP and the folder you want to share.

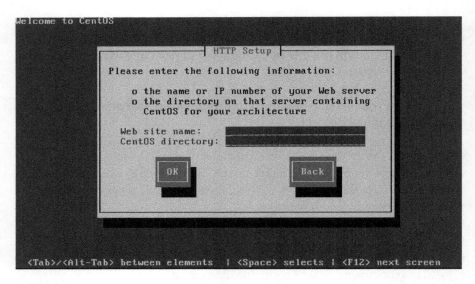

In the **Web site name** field type the IP address of your configured HTTP server and in the **CentOS directory** field type **/install**

You'll know that everything was configure correctly if after selecting **OK**, in the next screen will start a GUI installation of your operating system.

Installing from Hard Drive

Installing your Linux® operating system from an internal hard drive suppose that you have already installed on your computer a functional operating system no matter if that would be a Microsoft product or a Unix based product.

In that existing operating system you will create a directory **/install.**

Be sure you have at least 6 GB available space on the hard drive to download your CD/DVD ISO image with your desired operating system.

Assuming that you have downloaded the ISO image into the **/install** directory you might want to verify it.

- From a terminal use the following command:

    md5sum CentOS-[version]-i386-bin-DVD.iso

The mirror used to download the ISO file will provide also the proper **MD5 checksum** in a separate **md5sum.txt** file.

Compare the value obtained after using the **md5sum** command with the value provided by the **md5sum.txt** file of the mirror you used for download. They must be the same!

Next insert your boot USB key or boot CD, reboot your computer, be sure to select the proper boot sequence in BIOS and when the **boot:** prompt appears type **linux askmethod**.

Proceed as in the previous examples and from the **Installation Method** screen select **Hard drive.**
The next screen will ask you to specify the partition and the directory that contains the ISO files.
If you did the right selection the installation will start with a GUI interface.

Observations
*When you'll install your favorite distribution the first screen you'll see is the one with the **boot:** prompt.*
*You can install in graphical mode by pressing **Enter,** you can install in text mode by typing **linux text**, you can boot into rescue mode by typing **linux rescue** or you can type **linux noprobe** if your system is not detecting your wired network card.*

This could happen mainly if you try to install your Linux® distribution on a Laptop. The program will load the module for the wired Ethernet card but sometimes the module won't work and more than that, it will cause a core dump halting your system.

*The **linux noprobe** command can help you solve this problem.*
When you'll type it, the installation displays a dialog box that gives you the opportunity to add devices.

*Press **Tab** to highlight the **Add Device** button and then press **Enter**.*
*The installation program will display a dialog box that prompts you to select a driver from a list. Select the driver for your network card, press **Enter** and then follow the instructions.*

All installation methods described in this chapter apply for all Red Hat®
Enterprise Linux® based distributions. I have demonstrated this by using the
CentOS distribution as an example.

The IP addresses used here were examples that you have to replace with
those supplied by your ISP.

Chapter 2.   Configuring partitions

Partitioning a hard drive means to divide a single hard drive into many logical drives. You would want to do this for different reasons:

- It will help you keep data separated and safe from one another in case of certain hard drive failures.
- It will limit data growth as long as users or applications can consume so much space on hard drive that your operating system won't have enough space left for it's own operations leading to a disaster.
- Increasing disk space efficiency.

The manufacturers of hard drives build this devices using one or more platters centered on the same spinning axis. By adding platters the capacity of the hard drive will increase.

Each platter has two sides so this means that there are two surfaces on each platter where the data is stored.

To read from or write to these platters it's used a device called **head** located on an arm that has a radial motion over the platter. Usually there are two heads mounted on the arm to cover both sides of one platter.

The information on each platter is stored in **tracks** that represents small concentric circular strips.

You can conclude that from geometrical point of view a **track** is a bi-dimensional object.

If the hard drive contains more than one platter on the axis, the **tracks** with the same number but on different platters will be part of the same three dimensional object called **cylinder**.

Because the **tracks** are concentric you can imagine that the **cylinders** will be concentric too.

Think about these **cylinders** as being part of a round cake. If you cut a slice of this "cake" you'll obtain a three dimensional object called **sector**.

But remember that each **sector** obtained this way contains parts of different **tracks**.

These parts are called **blocks** representing the smallest geometrical breakdown of a disk and also the smallest amount of data which can be written to or read from a disk (usually 512 bytes).

Blocks are defined by specifying a certain **cylinder**, **sector** and **head**. The term **head** is also used to name a side of a platter.

Knowing this, now we can say that partitioning a hard drive means creating a sequence of cylinders representing all **sectors** that could be read by all **heads** with one movement of the arm.

Linux® uses a special nomenclature to refer to hard drive partitions. They are represented by **device files** located in **/dev.**
A device file could be **type c** - character device (devices that do not use the buffer cache), or **type b** - block device (devices that use the buffer cache).

All disks will be represented in Linux only as **block devices.**
Usually a computer has two IDE (Integrated Drive Electronics) or EIDE (Enhanced IDE) controllers and each can have two drives connected to it.
Given this situation, by convention, Linux® will name them :
- **/dev/hda** - the first drive (master drive) on the first IDE controller
- **/dev/hdb** - the second drive (slave drive) on the first IDE controller
- **/dev/hdc** - the first (master drive) on the second IDE controller
- **/dev/hdd** - the second (slave drive) on the second IDE controller

Each of these drives can be configured as primary, extended, logical and swap partition.

On a hard drive you can configure only 4 primary partitions and any of these can contain the boot files of your operating system.
One of the four primary partitions can be configured as an extended partition that will contain up to 12 logical partitions.

In order to write files on an extended partition you must configure at least one logical partition on it.
The first logical partition configured on any drive will be partition number 5.

Examples:
        /dev/hda5 - the first logical partition on hda drive
        /dev/hdd8 - the fourth logical partition on hdd drive
        /dev/hdc6 - the second logical partition on hdc drive

SATA (Serial AT Attachment) or SCSI (Small Computer System Interface) drives follow a similar pattern, Linux® naming them **/dev/sda**, **/dev/sdb**, etc.

The easiest way to create partitions is using **Disk Druid** during the installation of your operating system. It will save you a lot of trouble but if ever you'll have to add a new hard drive and re-organize the space on your hard drives, then you'll have to use **fdisk** or **parted** utilities.

Important observation
Once again I remind you to use virtual machines to practice any configuration. If you'll practice using the aforementioned utilities on your day by day system, a mistake will lead to a catastrophic lost of important data.

Assuming that you have a system running on a virtual machine already, be sure that it's enough space left on disk to practice configuring different partitions. If you use a virtual machine you can create fast and easy some virtual hard drives using the configuration menu of the program.

Creating partitions

Before starting to create partitions you must have in your mind two important things:
1. What you'll want the system to be dedicated for.
2. Linux uses **Filesystem Hierarchy Standard** (**FHS**) to organize files in directories.

Briefly I'll explain the basic **Filesystem Hierarchy Standard** directories.

/	The **root** directory. Always named / (slash) holds all other directories in all Linux® filesystems.
/bin	Essential command binaries. This directory holds all necessary files to start and maintain your system running in single user mode. Do not mount it separately.
/boot	The directory that holds the startup files and your system's kernel. By default it has 100MB.
/dev	Contains files that represent peripheral devices on your system: disk drives, CD/DVD-Rom drives, floppy drives, printers, etc. Do not mount it separately.

/etc   Directory that holds most basic configuration files of your machine. An important subdirectory is **/etc/passwd** that gives you information about users who have permission to use the machine.

/home   Contains the home directory for every user (except user root). Every user's home directory will appear as a subdirectory of **/home.**
                      Recommended to be mounted separately.

/lib   Shared libraries directory. Contains libraries for kernel and different utilities. Do not mount it separately.

/lost+found   This directory contains recovered or partial recovered files placed here after your system was rebooted in case of an improper shutdown or crush. Each partition has it's own **/lost+found** directory.

/media   Directory used by the system as a mount point for different removable media. Some other Linux® distributions use **/mnt** directory for the removable media to be mounted in.

/misc   Standard mount point for local directories.

/net   Standard mount point for network directories.

/opt   Directory for additional/optional installed software files.

/proc   Contains information about running processes related to kernel.

/root   Home directory for the Superuser named root.

/sbin   Essential system binaries. Contains utilities used for system administration.

/selinux   If SELinux is enabled and runs in Permissive or Enforced mode, this directory will hold the currently settings for it.

/srv	Data for services provided by the system.
/sys	Device pseudofilesystem.
/tmp	Directory that contains temporary files. The Red Hat® Enterprise Linux® based distributions will remove (by default) periodically data stored in this directory. You can mount it separately.
/usr	Stores programs accessible to all users including system administration commands and utilities. Can be mounted separately.
/var	Variable data is stored in this directory including logs, spool files and temporary e-mail files. It is recommended to be mounted separately.
swap	Linux swap space extends the amount of RAM on your computer. To prevent too many programs or data for using computer's RAM the kernel will try to place them in the swap space on your hard drive so the performances of your system won't be compromised. It's better to consider the swap space as emergency memory rather than extra memory because up to this moment accessing computer's RAM is still faster than accessing computer's hard drive.

If you choose to partition your hard drive when installing your distribution using Disk Druid, you should know that by default Red Hat® Enterprise Linux® based distributions will create three partitions also formating them with the default **ext3** filesystem:

- **/boot**
- **/**
- **swap**

There's nothing wrong with this type of partitioning and your system will work just fine if you choose it, but remember that accidents may occur and in this case a system crash would be fatal for your valuable data.

What is a filesystem?

The method for storing, manipulating, organizing and retrieving data from computer files represents a **filesystem**.

There are many types of filesystems.
Briefly I remind that Linux® supports many different filesystems but commonly used are ext2, ext3, swap, JFS, ReiserFS, xfs filesystems. Microsoft Windows® products use FAT and NTFS filesystems while MAC OS® X uses HFS Plus journaling filesystem.

The standard filesystem for CD-Rom is ISO 9660.

Red Hat® Enterprise Linux® based distributions use by default the **ext3** (Third Extended Filesystem) filesystem with journaling features.

In a journaling filesystem, changes are logged to a journal before committing them to the filesystem.
In case of system crush or power failure recovery is fast consisting in replaying the changes from this journal until the filesystem is valid again.

There are many ways you can partition the hard drive depending on the space available or the purpose you have in mind for your system to be dedicated to.

A common scheme of partitioning for a home computer would look like this:

/boot	- Usually 100MB large.
/var	- If you have enough space on disk make it no more than 3GB. That would be enough to hold the **/var/ log** directory.
swap	- Depends of your computer architecture. Without being a rule, use for swap the double amount of the computer's RAM but no more than 2GB. To improve performances split and scatter swap over all disks.
/	- Configure root partition with at least 6GB.
/home	- You can assign the rest of the remaining space on disk to user's home partition.

If you want your system to be a server you can use the same partitioning scheme as in the example used for a home computer but probably you'll want to allocate some more space for the **/var** directory and also to limit the **/tmp** and **/usr** directories to a certain amount of space.

In time, your experience and needs will help you choose the best partitioning scheme suitable for your computer.

Creating partitions using the fdisk utility

Exercise
You have installed a new hard drive that needs to be partitioned and you plan to use the following partition scheme:

- one primary partition of 512MB
- one logical partition of 2GB
- one swap partition of 256MB

• From a terminal (you have to be superuser in order to do this) type:

fdisk -l

The command returns a response similar to the following:

```
Disk /dev/sda: 10.7 GB, 10737418240 bytes
255 heads, 63 sectors/track, 1305 cylinders
Units = cylinders of 16065 * 512 = 8225280 bytes
```

Device	Boot	Start	End	Blocks	Id	System
/dev/sda1	*	1	13	104391	83	Linux
/dev/sda2		14	650	5116702+	83	Linux
/dev/sda3		651	777	1020127+	83	Linux
/dev/sda4		778	1305	4241130	5	Extended
/dev/sda5		778	1032	2048256	83	Linux
/dev/sda6		1033	1121	714861	82	Linux swap/
Solaris						

```
Disk /dev/sdb: 6442 MB, 6442450944 bytes
255 heads, 63 sectors/track, 783 cylinders
Units = cylinders of 16065 * 512 = 8225280 bytes
```

From this example you can see that the hard drive that needs to be partitioned is **/dev/sdb.**

- Type from a terminal :

  fdisk /dev/sdb then press **Enter**

You'll be instructed to press **m** for help and after you did so you should see
the complete list of options like this:

```
Command (m for help): m
Command action
      a      toggle a bootable flag
      b      edit bsd disklabel
      c      toggle the dos compatibility flag
      d      delete a partition
      l      list known partition types
      m      print this menu
      n      add a new partition
      o      create a new empty DOS partition table
      p      print the partition table
      q      quit without saving changes
      s      create a new empty Sun disklabel
      t      change a partition's system id
      u      change display entry units
      v      verify a partition table
      w      write table to dick and exit
      x      extra functionality (experts only)
```

- Press **p** to review the entries in the partition table

- Press **n** to create a new partition

You'll be instructed to specify what kind of partition do you want to create.
In this example you want to create first the primary partition. For that press **p**.

- Introduce the partition number. In this example I selected **1**

- Specify the first cylinder. Press **Enter** to select the first cylinder

- Specify the last cylinder or the desired size. The size you want is
  512MB so type **+512M**

```
Command (m for help): p
Disk /dev/sdb: 6442 MB, 6442450944 bytes
255 heads, 63 sectors/track, 783 cylinders
Units = cylinders of 16065 * 512 = 8225280 bytes


        Device   Boot  Start    End    Blocks   Id  System

Command (m for help): n
Command action
      e       extended
      p       primary partition (1-4)
p
Partition umber (1-4): 1
First cylinder (1-783, default 1):
Using default value 1
Last cylinder or +size or +sizeM or +sizeK (1-783,default
783):+512M

Command (m for help):
```

- To save your settings press **w** and then **Enter**

- Analyze the content of the **/proc/partitions** directory to see if your new created partition is shown:

  cat /proc/partitions

- Type **partprobe** and then **Enter** to "convince" the kernel to use the new partition table.

- Analyze again the **/proc/partitions** directory to see the changes:

  cat /proc/partitions

The primary partition having 512MB is created.
Now it's time to create a filesystem on it in order to write on this partition.

- Type the following command:
  mkfs.ext3 -L test /dev/sdb1

The command will create an **ext3** filesystem on the partition and also will apply the label (using the **-L** operator) **test** on it.

- Check your work by typing:

    blkid | grep test

The command should display something similar to :

```
/dev/sdb1: LABEL="test" UUID="275faabaa-876e-8cef-742fc41a88ef"
SEC_TYPE="ext2" TYPE="ext3"
```

- Open and edit with a text editor the **/etc/fstab** file introducing a new line containing information about your new created partition so next time when you boot the system it will be automatically mounted:

```
        LABEL=test    /opt     ext3 defaults      1  2
```

Take a look at the last line of the table. Be sure to maintain spaces between the table's columns.

```
LABEL=/            /              ext3      defaults        1  1
LABEL=/home        /home          ext3      defaults        1  2
LABEL=/var         /var           ext3      defaults        1  2
LABEL=/boot        /boot          ext3      defaults        1  2
tmpfs              /dev/shm       tmpfs     defaults        0  0
devpts             /dev/pts       devpts    gid=5,mode=620  0  0
sysfs              /sys           sysfs     defaults        0  0
proc               /proc          proc      defaults        0  0
LABEL=SWAP-sda6    swap           swap      defaults        0  0
LABEL=test         /opt           ext3      defaults        1  2
```

- Time to mount your partition into your desired directory (in this example I have chosen to mount it in **/opt** directory as you can see in **/etc/fstab**) and check your work.

    mount -a   will mount all partitions
    mount | grep "opt" or **mount -l**   to see all mounted partitions

- Reboot your system and check if your partition is mounted:

    df -l or **df -h**

```
[root@localhost ~]# df -h
Filesystem   Size        Used    Avail      Use%       Mounted on
/dev/sda2    4.8G        1.9G    2.6G       43%        /
/dev/sda3    965M        18M     898M       2%         /home
/dev/sda5    1.9G        152M    1.7G       9%         /var
/dev/sda1    99M         11M     83M        12%        /boot
tmpfs        252M        0M      252M       0%         /dev/shm
/dev/sdb1    479M        11M     444M       3%         /opt
```

What is /etc/fstab ?

The file **/etc/fstab** is a configuration file where Linux stores information about all mounted filesystems.
As you can see the information is organized per lines and columns.
Each line refers to one filesystem.
Let's analyze the first line in my **/etc/fstab**.

```
LABEL=/              /                    ext3    defaults        1   1
```

It shows information about **/dev/sda2.**
How do I know this ? Just take a closer look to the output returned by the **df -h**
command and compare it with the first line in my **/etc/fstab** file.
Also you have noticed that there are six columns in **/etc/fstab**.

First column — lists the device to be mounted. In this case, running the **e2label /dev/sda2** command the response will be : / This means that the device **/dev/sda2** is labeled as / (**LABEL=/**).

Second column — indicates the mount point for the filesystem (/)

Third column — shows the type of the filesystem on the device (**ext3**)

Fourth column — mount options (**default**). Using the **defaults** option, you'll establish in fact the following set of options for the filesystem:

rw — the partition is mounted read-write
suid — setuid or setgid are permitted on the filesystem.
dev — access to block devices and character devices permitted on the filesystem.

exec	- binaries allowed to be executed on the filesystem.
auto	- the filesystem is mounted automatically at boot or when the **mount -a** command is issued.
nouser	- only root can mount the filesystem
async	- I/O to the filesystem is done asynchronously.

There are many other options you can use to mount your filesystem. Consult the man pages (**man mount**) for detailed information.

Fifth column   - establishes the dump value. This can be **0** or **1**. If the value is set to **1** data will be automatically saved to disk by the **dump** command when exiting Linux. If the value is set to **0** or missing the **dump** command will assume that filesystem doesn't need to be dumped.

Sixth column   - indicates the order the **fsck** command checks the filesystem during the boot process. The values are **0**, **1** and **2**. The **0** value indicates that the filesystem doesn't need to be checked during the boot process. Use this value for removable media. Set to **1** for the root filesystem and **2** for the others filesystems. If no value is set then the **fsck** command will assume that the filesystem doesn't need to be checked.

Following similar steps you'll create the logical partition.

- fdisk -l /dev/sdb
- Type **n** to create a new partition.
- Type **e** for creating first an extended partition. Remember the discussion about extended and logical partitions.
- You'll be asked to enter the number of the partition you want to be extended. Remember that partition number **1** was already created (/**dev/sdb1**) as primary, so your options now are **2**, **3**, or **4**. Assuming you have chosen partition **2**, press **Enter**.

- When asked about the first cylinder press **Enter** to use default.
- For last cylinder type **+2000M** and press **Enter.**

You have created now an extended 2GB partition but in order to use it you must create a logical partition with a filesystem on it.

- Type **n** to add a new partition.
- Now you're prompted to type **l** for creating a logical partition or to type **p** to create a primary partition. Notice that your logical partition will be partition number 5. Remember again the previous discussion about logical partitions. For the purpose of this exercise type **l** and then **Enter**.
- Select the default value for the first cylinder by pressing **Enter**.
- Select the default value for the last cylinder (you don't need to type +200M again) by pressing **Enter**.
- Save your settings and exit by typing **w.**
- Check your work with **partprobe** and **cat /proc/partitions** commands.

To create a filesystem on a logical partition follow these steps:

- From a terminal type:

mkfs.ext3 -L logic /dev/sdb5

The command will create an ext3 filesystem named **logic** on the first logical partition (partition number 5) of **/dev/sdb**.
I've used the label "logic" here but you can use a different name for it.

- Check if the label was applied:

blkid | grep logic

- Edit **/etc/fstab** introducing a new line with information about the logical partition you've created.
The line should indicate that the partition named **logic** is mounted in **/mnt** (for example) using the **default** options and contains an **ext3** filesystem on it.

```
LABEL=logic    /mnt    ext3    defaults    1    2
```

- Mount all partitions:

mount -a

- Verify mounted partitions with the following command:

mount | grep "mnt" or **mount -l**

- Reboot your computer and then use the following command to see if all partitions are mounted:

  df -h or **df -l**

The last part of the exercise consists in creating a 256MB **swap** partition on the same **/dev/sdb** device.

- From a terminal use again the **fdisk** command:

  fdisk /dev/sdb

- Type **n** for adding a new partition.
- If you choose **swap** to be a primary partition the options left for it are either partition 3 or partition 4.
- Assuming you have chosen partition 3, then type **3** and then **Enter**.
- Select the first and the last cylinder as described earlier for the other partitions.
- Type **m** for help and read the explanations for **t** command.
- When you type **t** remember that you have chosen swap to be partition 3. At this moment type **3.**
- You have to change the hex code for **swap**. Notice that when you created the other partitions, the hex code for them was **83**.
- Type **L** to obtain the list with associated hex codes as instructed.
- In this list you'll find **82** the associated hex code for **swap**.
- Type **82** and then **Enter**.
- Save and exit with **w** command.
- Use again **partprobe** to "convince" the kernel to read the new partition table and check your work with **cat /proc/partitions.**

The **swap** partition is now created and needs to be formated.

- **mkswap -L newswap /dev/sdb3**
  This command formats the partition to a Linux swap filesystem and also, by using option **-L** will name it "**newswap**". Of course, you can use any other name for it.
- Use **blkid** command to check your work.
- Edit **/etc/fstab** introducing a new line containing information about your new created swap partition:

```
LABEL=newswap swap  swap     defaults   0  0
```

- Mount the new created swap partition with **swapon -a** command
- Verify your work with **swapon -s** command.
  The output of **swapon -s** command will show all existing swap partitions.

To delete a partition first unmount it using the **umount** command and then press **d** in the **fdisk** command menu.

For example if you want to delete **/dev/sdb1** (labeled "test") created earlier :
- **umount /dev/sdb1**
- **fdisk /dev/sdb**
- Press **m** for help
- Press **d** to delete the partition. You'll be asked what's the number of the partition you want to delete. In our case is partition 1
- Press **w** to save and exit
- **partprobe**
- Use **cat /proc/partitions** to see the changes

Observation

You have noticed the -L operator associated with mkfs and mkswap commands. If you include this operator, the mentioned commands will create the desired filesystem on the specified partition and also will apply a label at once. So consider using it if you want to save time.
Also you can practice the use of tune2fs and e2label commands for creating a filesystem and labeling your partitions.

Assuming that you have already created your primary partition from this example try now to use the aforementioned commands to create an ext3 filesystem and label it.
Follow this steps:

- **tune2fs -j /dev/sda1**
- **e2label /dev/sda1 test**
- **blkid | grep test**
- Edit **/etc/fstab** and introduce the mentioned line:

```
LABEL=test        /opt        ext3        defaults      1   2
```

- **mount -a**
- **mount | grep "opt"**

Remember to use **man** or **info** if you want to find details about the commands I have used in this chapter.

Software RAID

RAID stands for Redundant Array of Independent Disks and helps you organize multiple disks into a large and high performance logical disk.

There are several levels of RAID software supported by Red Hat Enterprise Linux distributions : RAID 0, RAID 1, RAID 4, RAID 5, RAID 6 and combinations of these (for example RAID 50 or RAID 01).

RAID 0 - known as "Stripping without parity", requires at least two hard disks and provides speed in reading and writing the disks but without data redundancy. The information is written simultaneously on both disks but if one disk in this array fails, all data from both disks will be lost.

RAID 1 - also known as "Mirrored without parity" uses two or sets of two disks to mirror data between disks. Data is written on one disk and then mirrored on the other disk so if one disk in this array is damaged the other disk (or the other pair of disks) will still hold the information.

RAID 4 - known as "Disk stripping with parity" requires at least three disks. Reading and writing data on disk are done the same way as for RAID 0 while the third disk holds the parity information necessary for data reconstruction.

RAID 5 - "Striped set with distributed parity" needs three or more disks as RAID 4 but in this case parity information is evenly distributed on all disks so if one disk fails data is reconstructed from the parity information on the remaining disks. In case of a drive failure in this array even if the performance of the whole array will decrease the data won't be lost and the system will run until the damaged disk is replaced. This feature makes RAID 5 to be the favorite choice.

RAID 6 - "Striped set with dual distributed parity" requires four or more disks and even if two disks fail, the array continues to operate.

Creating a RAID array

Exercise
Using the virtual machine configure three virtual hard drives with some free space assuming that you want to create a **level 5** RAID array for **/home** directory.

Of course the easiest way to create this array is using the GUI interface during the installation but for the purpose of the exercise I'll use the terminal commands to create this array.

Assuming that **/dev/sdb**, **dev/sdc** and **/dev/sdd** are the devices you'll work with, here are the necessary steps:

- I'll use the fdisk command again, so from a terminal type:

  fdisk /dev/sdb

- Type **n** to create a new partition and supposing that you want this partition to be primary, type **p.**
- Establish the first and last cylinder for this partition.
- When finished, type **m** for help and then type **t** to change partition's ID.
- You'll be instructed to type **L** for the list of hex codes. You'll find that the hex code for RAID is **fd.**
- Type **fd,** then **w** and press **Enter** to save your settings.
- Type **partprobe** and **Enter** so the kernel will use the new partition table.

Follow the same steps to configure **/dev/sdc** and **/dev/sdd**

- Now you have to create a **level 5** RAID device called **/dev/md0** and formatting it with an ext3 filesystem so from a terminal type:

mdadm -C /dev/md0 --level=5 --raid-device=3 /dev/sdb1 /dev/sdc1 /dev/sdd1

- Verify your work**:**

  cat /proc/mdstat

- Apply the ext3 filesystem:

  mkfs.ext3 /dev/md0

- Edit **/etc/fstab** inserting a line containing information about your new RAID device:

```
/dev/md0           /home ext3     defaults      1      2
```

Notice that the mount point for the RAID device is **/home** as I have specified at the beginning of this exercise.

- Mount all partitions:

  mount -a

Observations
You can practice creating RAID arrays using the same hard drive or even using an USB key but you have to remember that in real life this would be a nonsense.

Whenever you'll want to delete a RAID partition, make sure that all data is saved and then unmount it prior to deletion.

Logical Volume Management

Logical Volume Management (or Logical Volume Manager or, simply LVM) is a method that helps you allocate, extend or reduce space on mass storage devices.
Using LVM you can allocate the extra space from one directory partition to another directory partition.
You can use LVM with a RAID array but remember that it doesn't provide redundancy itself so it can't be used as a substitute for RAID.
LVM also allows you to create read-write snapshots if you apply copy-on-write to each logical extent.
However it has some disadvantages.
The boot process might be a little slower and if you try to recover your system in case an accident occurred it will be very difficult especially when the system itself and important tools are part of a logical volume.

Creating a new LVM

It's a process that involves three steps: first you have to create a physical volume, then you need to assign the space to a volume group and finally allocate the available space on a volume group to a logical volume.

Creating a physical volume

- **Use the fdisk -l** command to display the device you'll use.
  For this exercise the device is **/dev/sdb**

  fdisk /dev/sdb

If **/dev/sdb** has no partition on it you can create for example two or more partitions.

Let's say that the **cat /proc/partitions** command shows for **/dev/sdb** two partitions: **/dev/sdb1** and **/dev/sdb2**.

- Press **t** to change partition's ID and then press **L** for the list of hex codes.
- You'll find that for physical volume the hex code is **8e**.
  Type **8e** then **Enter.**
- Type **w** then **Enter** to save your settings.

- Type **pvcreate /dev/sdb1**
  Type **pvcreate /dev/sdb2**

- Verify the existence of your physical volumes by typing **pvs** from a terminal.

Creating a volume group

- Type **vgcreate vgrp01 /dev/sdb1 /dev/sdb2**
  I have named **vgrp01** this new created volume group. You can use any name you want for it.
- Verify the existence of your volume group by typing **vgs**

Creating a logical volume

You can allocate the entire space for this logical volume or you can allocate only a chunk for example 512MB.

- If you want to allocate the entire space for this logical volume type:

  lvcreate -L [total_amount_of_space] -n /dev/vgrp01/lvol01

Replace the expresion **[total_amount_of_space]** with a number that reflects your current total available space in MB.

- If you want to allocate only a chunk (in my example) 512MB, type:

  lvcreate -L 512M -n /dev/vgrp01/lvol01

The command will create a logical volume named **lvol01** heaving **512MB** Use any name you want to refer to your logical volume.

- Verify your work by typing **lvs**

You've created a LVM but in order to use it you have to add a filesystem on it.

- Use the **mkfs.ext3** command to add an ext3 filesystem to your LVM :

mkfs.ext3 /dev/vgrp01/lvol01

- If you want to label your logical volume then issue the same command using the **-L** operator:

mkfs.ext3 -L logic_volum /dev/vgrp01/lvol01

I have used the name **logic_volume** as an example. Use any other name you want for it.

- Edit **/etc/fstab** introducing a line containing information about your logical volum:

```
/dev/vgrp01/lvol01   /home/user_name   ext3   default   1 2
```

If you have applied the aforementioned label on LVM the line will be:

```
LABEL=logic_volume   /home/user_name   ext3   default   1 2
```

- Save your settings in **/etc/fstab** and mount all partitions by typing from a terminal:

mount -a

- Reboot your system and notice the changes using **df -h** command.

What if you want to extend the logical volume?

Assuming that you added a new hard drive or still have unused space left and you want to add for example 2GB, you will use the **vgextend** and **lvextend** commands.

- **Save any data in /home/user_name**
- **umount /dev/vgrp01/lvol01**

For example on your new added hard drive **/dev/sdc** you have created **/dev/sdc1** partition having 2GB and you want to add this space to your existing logical volume **lvol01.** To do this, follow these steps:

- **pvcreate /dev/sdc1**

- **vgextend /dev/vgrp01 /dev/sdc1**

The command will extend the volume group **vgrp01** to your new partition /**dev/sdc1.**

- Check your work with the **vgs** command:

lvextend -L 2.5G -n /dev/vgrp01/lvol01

Your new logical volume obtained this way will contain 512M of space created previously with /**dev/sdb1** and /**dev/sdb2** plus your new 2G (2000M) added partition device /**dev/sdc1.**

- Verify your work with the **lvs** command:

If you want to find the devices that are part of the new extended logical volume and also how space is managed now, issue the **pvs** command.

- Apply a filesystem:

mkfs.ext3 -L new_logic_volume /dev/vgrp01/lvol01

Notice that I have created again an **ext3** filesystem on the extended logical volume and I've labeled it **new_logic_volume**. I've used this label just to underline the changes in this example, but you can use any other label you want.

- Edit /**etc/fstab** adding the new information about the extended logical volume:

```
LABEL=new_logic_volume  /home/user_name  ext3  defaults  1 2
```

- Mount all partitions:

mount -a

- Reboot your system and notice the changes with **df -h** command.

How about removing a logical volume?

To remove a logical volume you'll save first any important data contained in that logical volume and then you have to unmount all directories associated with the respective logical volume.

Using the previous example, you'll need to follow these steps:

- **Save any data in /home/user_name**
- **umount /dev/vgrp01/lvol01**
- **lvremove /dev/vgrp01/lvol01**
- Verify your work with **lvs.** If everything was done right the output of **lvs** command will confirm your changes.

- You can go further if you want by removing also the volume group **vgrp01**:

  vgremove /dev/vgrp01

Observation
LVM presents a multitude of commands regarding the management of physical volumes, volume groups and logical volumes as you can see in the following tables:

Table 1

Physical Volume Commands	Description
pvcreate	Creates a physical volume on a partition
pvchange	Changes attributes of a physical volume
pvmove	Moves a physical volume on another partition
pvremove	Removes a physical volume
pvresize	Resize physical volumes
pvdisplay	Displays a list of configured physical volumes
pvs ; pvscan	Lists physical volumes associated with volume group if they were already configured so.

Table 2

Volume Group Commands	Description
vgcreate	Creates a volume group from at least two already configured physical volumes
vgchange	Changes attributes of a volume group
vgmerge	Merges a volume group into an existing one
vgrename	Renames an existing volume group
vgreduce	Reduces a volume group by removing one or more unused physical volumes from it.
vgremove	Removes a volume group not assigned to a logical volume
vgextend	Adds one or more initialized physical volumes to an existing volume group
vgcfgbackup	Allows metadata backup of a volume group in a text file
vgcfgrestore	Restores backed up metadata of a volume group from the text file produced by the **vgcfgbackup** command
vgexport	Makes volume groups unknown to the system preparing them for an eventual import
vgimport	Import the unknown volume groups making them known to the system after their physical volumes were moved from another machine
vgconvert	Converts the format of a volume group metadata into another provided format, so metadata will fit into the same space
vgmknodes	Recreates the volume group directory and the special files of the logical volume. If these special files are missing, they will be created and the unused ones will be deleted.
vgs ; vgscan	Scans and lists basic information about volume group

Table 3

Logical Volume Commands	Description
lvcreate	Creates a logical volume in an existing volume group
lvchange	Changes attributes of a logical volume
lvrename	Renames a logical volume
lvreduce	Reduces the size of a logical volume
lvremove	Removes a logical volume
lvresize	Resizes a logical volume
lvextend	Extends a logical volume to a desired size
lvconvert	Converts a linear logical volume to a mirror logical volume or to a snapshot of linear volume and vice versa
lvdisplay	Displays attributes of a logical volume (size, status, snapshot information, etc.)
lvs ; lvscan	Scans and lists basic information about logical volume

*Don't forget to consult the **man** pages referring to all **pv***, **vg***, **lv*** group of commands if you need detailed information about descriptions and options of these commands.*

For creating a LVM or/and a RAID array you can use the graphical tools provided once you're installing your operating system into your computer. In case you'll want to add a new hard drive to your computer you still can use the graphical tools provided by LVM to create a new logical volume but if you will want to create a new RAID array, then you have to use the console and the utilities described in this chapter.
*You can practice also creating LVM with the GUI LVM tool, either using the **system-config-lvm** command from a terminal, or opening **System – Administration – Logical Volume Management.***
Practice with both methods and in time you'll decide which one is suitable for you.

Chapter 3. Managing users, groups and permissions in Linux ®

Linux uses three basic types of accounts:

- administrative – root
- regular – users
- service – mail, Apache, Squid, Samba, etc

The **root** account is automatically created during the installation process and allows you to manage the entire system.
The root's home directory is **/root**.

Managing services or modifying configuration files requires login as **root**, so be careful what changes you want to make in your system in order to avoid a catastrophic loss of data or worse, such a damaged system that recovery may be impossible.

Users accounts are created by the administrator of the system (root) or by the user that has administrative rights over the system.

User's home directory is created in /**home/user_name** where **user_name** is the name of the user allowed to use the system.

When **root** adds a new user in the system, that user will have, by default, enough privileges to perform basic operations as creating, moving, removing, storing files in their home directories.
By default, users don't have access to important configuration files, can't access each other's home directory modifying or deleting each other's file unless the administrator of the system (root) sets the appropriate permissions for this.

Service account is used by a specific service as mail, Apache, Squid, Samba, etc. to interact with your system.

Adding a new user

You can add users and create passwords for them from a command line, or using the tools provided by GUI.

The fastest way to add a new user is using the command line and the appropriate commands.

For example, if you want to add a new user called **user1**, from a terminal type:

> **useradd user1**
> **passwd user1**

At this moment you'll have to introduce twice the password you have chosen for the user named **user1.**

But what happens in fact when you introduce these commands from a terminal?

The system will edit automatically four important files (**/etc/passwd, /etc/group, /etc/shadow, /etc/gshadow**), assigns the **/home/user1** directory as the home directory for **user1** and copies a default set of environment files from **/etc/skel** directory into the **/home/user1** directory.

This environment files are hidden (their names start with a dot) and you can list all of them issuing the **ls -al /home/user1** or **ls -al /etc/skel** commands.

If your last added user was **user1** then the last line of the **/etc/passwd** file will contain an entry like this:

```
user1:x:500:500::/home/user1:/bin/bash
```

To check the content of the **/etc/passwd** file, from a terminal (as root) type **cat /etc/passwd.**
You will notice that all entries in **/etc/passwd** are organized per lines and each line has seven fields as in the following table:

Table 4

Field Name	Description	Example
User name	This is the the name of the user allowed to log in into the system.	user1
Password	The password used by user1 to login.	x
User ID	Is a unique ID number assigned by your distribution for each user of your system. By default, starts with 500.	500
Group ID	The ID number that designates one group to one or more users. By default starts with 500	500
User information	This field is blank by default but you can edit it by adding some information about the user such as user's real name, user's e-mail address, etc.	: :
Home directory	The field specifies the location of user's home directory.	/home/user1
Login shell	Red Hat Enterprise Linux based distributions assign by default the / **bin/bash** shell for users but this shell can be changed to any other installed shell using the **chsh** command.For example: **chsh -s /bin/ksh** or **chsh -s /bin/zsh**, etc.	/bin/bash

Observations

*In the **Password** field you might have an x which indicates that user's encrypted password is in /etc/shadow file, an * indicating in this case that the account is disabled, or a group of numbers and letters representing the encrypted password.*

You have decided to install and use Linux because you were convinced by the multitude of advantages this operating system provides including security. A secure system starts with choosing passwords difficult to crack by someone using programs made for this purpose.

When creating a password, do not use simple combinations of letters and/or numbers that may contain someone's name, birth date, phone number, etc. If you feel that you just ran out of inspiration in choosing a good password you can use the following command for generating a random group of numbers and letters to be used as a password:

cat /dev/urandom | tr -cd "a-zA-Z0-9" | fold -w 6 | head

Don't be scared by the length of this expression. All you have to remember is that the expression includes four simple and probably known commands calling the /dev/urandom device.
In other words, with this command you "call" /dev/urandom device but you want the "answer" from it to be translated (tr -cd command) using all letters of the English alphabet (including the capital ones) and all numbers from 0 to 9.
More than that, you want each line of the "answer" wrapped (fold command) to fit in a specified width (-w 6 means groups of 6 characters) and finally you want to read only the first 10 lines (by default head/tail commands will list the first/last 10 lines of a file) of the "answer".
Try this command including all characters provided by your keyboard generating groups longer than 6 characters.

To delete an user account use **userdel user_name** command from a terminal. For example if you want to remove **user1** from your system type :

userdel -r user1

The command will remove the user's account and also his home directory and all files includer there. If you don't insert the **-r** operator the user account will be deleted but his home directory (**/home/user1**) will remain in your system.
Consult the man pages for detailed options (**man userdel**).

Another method for adding users to your computer is using the graphical user interface (GUI). All you have to do is to select **System** then **Administration** where you'll click on **Users and Groups**.

In the menu that opens click on **Add User** button.

Notice that by default the system will create a home directory for user (option **Create home directory** is checked), a login shell (**Login shell** checked to be **/bin/bash**) and assigns a group for your user (option **Create a private group for user** is checked).

This brings in discussion the **/etc/group** file. To view the content of **/etc/group** file type **cat /etc/group** from a terminal.

The information in the **/etc/group** is organized similar as in the **/etc/passwd** file but in this case only four fields are defined:

```
user1:x:500:
```

In the following table I'll describe these fields:

Table 5

Field Name	Description	Example
Group Name	The name of the group assigned to a specific user.	user1
Password	The password used by the user to login.	x
Group ID	The ID number that designates one group to one or more users. By default starts with 500.	500
Group Members	This field presents the users that are members of the respective group.	Blank field indicates that **user1** is the only member of this group

Observation
*In the **Password** field you might have an x which indicates that the encrypted password is in /etc/gshadow file, or a group of numbers and letters representing the encrypted password.*

If you want to delete an user select the desired user from the menu and click **Delete.**

Notice that you'll be asked if you want the user's home directory along with all files included to be deleted too. This is the equivalent of the **userdel -r user1** command.

To add or remove a group, from a terminal type **groupadd group_name** or **groupdel group_name** where **group_name** is the desired group you want to add/remove.

If you prefer the GUI tools to add a group click on **System – Administration – Users and Groups** and in the menu click on **Add Group.**
To remove a group just click on **Groups** tab, select the desired group to be removed and then click **Delete** in the menu.

Observation
Sometimes you'll want to add a new user into your system but you don't want to create a home directory for the user and also you don't want to assign a group.

The fastest method to do this is to use the command line by typing :

> *useradd -Mn new_user*

*For more options read the man pages referring to **useradd** command (**man useradd**).*

A closer look at **User Manager** utility reveals more settings available after you have created an account.
Select an user click on **Properties** button and in the new set of options click **Account Info** tab.

By activating **Enable account expiration** you can set the expiration date of the account.

Further more, by clicking on **Password Info** tab you can set the password expiration date by checking the box **Enable password expiration.**

And finally, if you want the selected user to be also a member of another group click the **Groups** tab for the next menu.

Notice that **user1** is already a member of user1's group and by checking the appropriate box, I have placed **user1** also in the group **wheel.**

Making **user1** also a member of the group **wheel** means that I allowed **user1** to access the **su** command.

Same result is obtained faster if from a terminal you type:

usermod -G wheel user1

When an user is assigned also to another group, in the **/etc/group** file the entry referring to that group reflects this fact too.
Given the example above, notice now that not only **root** is a member of the group **wheel** but also **user1** is affiliated to the group **wheel.**

```
wheel:x:10:root,user1
```

Using different operators (**man usermod**), the **usermod** command modifies accounts reflecting the changes in **/etc/shadow** file.
For example if you want user1's account to expire at 23rd of August 2015, from a terminal type :

usermod -e 2015-08-23 user1

Also you can set the expiration date of user1's password by using **chage** command or **User Manager**.

If you want to set the expiration date for user1's password to be 1st of December 2015, type from a terminal :

chage -E 2015-12-01 user1

Consult the manual for the **chage** command because there are many other options associated with this command.

Same result you'll see in the **/etc/shadow** file if in **User Manager** you select **user1,** click on **Properties** and then click on **Password Info**.

Let's analyze the answer returned by the **cat /etc/shadow** command regarding **user1:**

```
user1:$1$7jqnWqAt$1bHUx8LrFvcIk9avLZsfP1:14333:0:99999:7::18497:
```

Explanations regarding the fields in the **/etc/shadow** file are presented in the following table:

Table 6

Field Name	Description	Example
User name	The field indicates the user's name	user1
Password	User's encrypted password (this is the meaning of **x** you see in **/etc/passwd**)	
Password history	Shows the date in number of days after 1st of January 1970, of the last password change	14333
Minimum days	The minimum number of days you must keep the password	0
Maximum days	The maximum number of days after which the password must be changed	99999
Warning days	A warning will be given with a certain number of days (seven in this case) before password expiration	7
Inactive account	The account will be inactive after a certain number of days since password expired. Not set in my example.	: :
Disable account	The account will be disabled after a certain number of days since password expired.	18497

Permitting regular users access to the su and sudo commands

Sometimes you might have to permit regular users to access the root account using their own passwords. This situation is met when you're not the only system administrator of the network.

To permit **user1** to access the root account follow these steps:

- From a terminal type:

  usermod -G wheel user1

The command will make **user1** a member of the **wheel** group

- Open with a text editor the **/etc/pam.d/su** file and remove the pound #
  character from in front of the following line :

```
auth            required         pam_wheel.so       use_uid
```

Doing this you make the **PAM** (Pluggable Authentication Modules) to look
for the group **wheel.**

Furthermore you'll want **user1** to gain access to administrative commands.

- From a teminal type:

  visudo

The command will open **/etc/sudoers** file in **vi** editor

- Navigate to the line root   ALL=(ALL)   ALL and beneath it
  introduce a new line referring to user1:

```
user1    ALL=(ALL)     ALL
```

If you activate the line %wheel   ALL=(ALL)   ALL, members of the group
wheel will gain access to all administrative commands but they will be
prompted for their own password.

Activating the line %wheel   ALL=(ALL)   NOPASSWD: ALL, members of
the **wheel** group will have access to all administrative commands but in this
case no password is required.

- Save settings and exit

- Login as **user1** and check your work by issuing from a terminal the
  following command for example:

  sudo /sbin/ifconfig

Depending of what option you have activated in **/etc/sudoers** file you'll be
prompted (or not) for **user1** password.

The **sudo /sbin/ifconfig** command was used here as an example. Logged in as **user1** now you have access to all administrative commands.

I have mentioned that when a new user is added, the system also copies a default set of environment files from **/etc/skel** into user's home directory. These files are invisible but you can list them by using the **-al** operators with the **ls** command.

From a terminal type **ls -al /etc/skel** or **ls -al /home/user1**
Depending of your configuration, many files are listed but I will analyze only three of them : **/etc/skel/. bash_logout**, **/etc/skel/.bash_profile** and **/etc/skel/.bashrc.**

The **.bash_logout** file is executed when exiting a bash shell by clearing for example the screen.

The **.bash_profile** file configures the bash startup environment.

The **.bashrc** file includes a list of aliases for commands you will want to run when starting a bash shell.
For example you want to create a new alias for the **eject** command that has some special features : when you type **eject** from a terminal, the CD/DVD-Rom will be opened and when for the second time **eject** command is introduced from the terminal the CD/DVD-Rom will be closed.

- Use a text editor to open the **/home/user1/.bashrc** file and add a new line that contains the following entry:

   alias eject='eject -T'

- Save your settings and exit

Now check your work typing from a terminal **eject** once. The CD/DVD ROM's tray should open and when the command is issued for the second time, the tray should close.

If you have a keyboard with multimedia features you'd probably like to assign certain commands to different keys (Play, Stop, Eject, etc) or combinations of keys in order to gain access and operate faster your Media Player, CD/DVD-Rom, Firefox, Thunderbird Mail, etc.

Considering the previous example, click on **System**, choose **Preferences** and then click on **Keyboard Shortcuts.** In the menu, navigate to **Sound** section and now you can establish what button or combination of buttons you'll want to use for opening the CD/DVD ROM without even typing the **eject** command from the terminal.

Changing ownership, permissions and attributes of files and directories

By default users can't access each other's files or directories. This is the basic protection method against accidentally deleting files.

I remind that only root can change a file's owner and only root or the owner can change a file's group.
The **chown** command will change file owner and group, while **chgrp** command will change only group ownership.
Consulting the man pages for these commands you'll find that the syntax

> **chgrp -R group_name file**

is identical to

> **chown group_name file**

In Linux, permissions may be : Read (**r**), Write (**w**), Execute (**x**), Set User ID or Set Group ID bit (**s**) and Sticky bit (**t**).

What are special permissions user ID bit, group ID bit and sticky bit?

This special permissions refers to the way an application or a file should be treated regarding the ownership or appurtenance of these.
When you set the **user ID bit (SUID)**, you will allow an application or file to run with privileges of the owner rather than the privileges of the user.
In other words, if you set the user ID bit to a script that normally runs under root privileges, that script will be executed also by a regular user because this way that regular user gains access to same privileges as root!

Same thing happens if you set the **group ID bit (SGID)** only that this time a regular user will run an application or a file with privileges of the group rather than privileges of the user.
This is useful when you want different users create and modify files in a certain common directory.

Back in the days, setting the **sticky bit** special permission meant that after executing an application, this was placed into swap so in case this application had to be used again the kernel would have moved it from swap to RAM increasing this way the access speed for the respective application.

Today this thing is less important considering the advanced technology used for building computers.
When the **sticky bit** is set on a directory, files inside that directory will be modified or deleted only by the owner of those files, the owner of the directory or superuser.

Permissions are changed with **chmod** command.
You can use the symbolic method to change permissions, the numeric method, or if you're logged in GUI you can right click on a file, select **Properties** from the menu, select **Permissions** tab and then modify **Folder Access** and **File access** for Owner, Group and Others sections as you wish.

Changing permissions using the symbolic method

Permissions described earlier are applied for users who own the files/directories (**u**), groups (**g**), or other users (**o**) by using operator "Plus" (**+**) when you want to add permission, or operator "Minus" (**-**) when you want to remove permission.

Examples:

      chmod ug+rwx,o-rw testfile

This means that I have granted (+) user and group (**ug**) read, write and execute permission (**rwx**) over the file named **testfile** and denied (-) read and write permission (**rw**) for others (**o**) over the same **testfile**.

      chmod a=rwx testfile

With this command I have assigned to all (**a**) categories (**u, g, o**) read, write and execute permission (**rwx**).

      chmod -R a+rwxst test_director

In this case I have assigned recurrently (the **-R** operator) to all categories read, write and execute permissions over the directory named **test_directory** and files contained by it. More than that I have set also recurrently special permissions **user ID bit (SUID)**, **group ID bit (GID)** and **sticky bit.**

Changing permissions using the numeric method

The numeric method uses a three digit mode number.
First digit specifies owner's permission, second digit specifies group's permission and the third digit specifies permission for others.
If special permissions have to be set, this is done by adding a supplementary digit in front of that specifying owner's permission.
Permissions are calculated by adding **4** for read, **2** for write and **1** for execute.
Special permissions use the same pattern : **4** for SUID bit, **2** for SGID bit and **1** for sticky bit.

Examples:

> **chmod 661 testfile**
> **chmod -R 2770 test_directory**

Observations
The sticky bit will be indicated with capital "T" instead of lower case "t" if it is set on a file or directory for which the execute (x) permission was not granted in the others (o) category.
Also capital "S" will be displayed instead of lower case "s" when SUID or SGID fails to be set.
Be careful when use SUID special permission on files owned by root otherwise your system might be compromised.

The default permission for directories is **777** minus **umask.**
To find the **umask** value for root, from a terminal login as root and type **umask**. You'll find this as being **022.**
Similar, if from a terminal you login as a non privileged user, and type **umask**, you'll find this value as being **002.**
Knowing this you can conclude that the default permission for root's directories is **755** (777 - 022 = 755) and the default permission for non-privileged user's directories is **775** (777 - 002 = 775)

For files, the default permission is the directory's default permission minus **execute** permission (**x**).

Considering this, root's files will have 644 permission and files of
non-privileged users will have 664 permission.

Observation
Changing umask's value from 022 to a more permissive value, for example
002 is done if from a terminal you type:

umask 002

*Reboot the computer and see what value will return the **umask's** command.*
Is it 022 again?
*This happens because the value of **umask** is defined in /etc/bashrc file which*
is read by the system at startup.
*The command that you used does not modify **umask**'s value in /etc/bashrc.*
*To make the change permanent, open with /etc/bashrc file with **vi** editor and*
replace accordingly.

Another method to protect files against accidental deletion or modifications
is changing the attributes of the file.
For example if you want to list the attributes of **/boot/grub/grub.conf** file
use the **lsattr** command:

lsattr /boot/grub/grub.conf

The output of this command will show that no attribute was specified for this file:

```
[root@localhost ~]# lsattr /boot/grub/grub.conf
------------- /boot/grub/grub.conf
```

Adding the immutable attribute to this file is possible by issuing the **chattr**
command.

chattr +i /boot/grub/grub.conf

To verify your work, type again **lsattr /boot/grub/grub.conf** and notice the
output:

```
[root@localhost ~]# lsattr /boot/grub/grub.conf
----i-------- /boot/grub/grub.conf
```

Try to delete or modify this file now and see what's happening!

To add an attribute to a file use the "Plus" (+) operator and to remove an attribute use the "Minus" (-) operator.
For more information about this command use the **man** pages (**man chattr**).

Sometime users need to share the content of specific directories, having access to specific files.
As a system administrator you'll need to establish special permissions over those files or directories so only users you want may have this privilege.

Exercise
Add the following users to your system: **user_a**, **user_b**, **user_c**
Create a common directory (**/home/share**) for all aforementioned users but only **user_a** and **user_b** to be able to access and edit the file named **test** (**/home/share/test**). Make sure **user_c** will be able only to read the **/home/share/test** file as any other files created in **/home/share** directory.
Any other users that you might add into your system must have no read, write or execute rights over the /home/share directory.

- First you have to create the **/home/share** directory
  As root, from a terminal type :

  mkdir /home/share

- Then create the **/home/share/test** file:

  touch /home/share/test

- In order to be able to share and modify files in **/home/share** directory you want **user_a** and **user_b** to be also part of a common group but you don't want any of these users to take control over this common group.
  If the common group's name will be **shared_group** and if you'll use a terminal, there are two methods to add these users to this group :

  a) You can use a text editor to edit the **/etc/group** file.
     Once this file opened press **G** to navigate at the bottom of it and then press **o** to add a new line.
     On this new line add the following entry but be sure it contains no empty spaces:

     ```
     shared_group:x:5000:user_a,user_b
     ```

b) You can use **groupadd** and **usermod** commands to obtain the same result:

groupadd shared_group
usermod -G shared_group user_a
usermod -G shared_group user_b

As an additional exercise try adding to your system the common group **shared_group** and then make **user_a** and **user_b** members of this group by using the graphical user interface.
Practicing with all three methods you'll decide for yourself which one is faster and easier to be used.

- Use **chown** command to change the ownership of the group **shared_group** so none of users will take control over this group:

chown nobody.shared_group /home/share
or
chown nobody:shared_group /home/share

No matter what syntax you'll use for introducing the command, you'll obtain the same result: the already existing group named **nobody** takes the ownership of the group named **shared_group** over the **/home/share** directory and all of the containing files.

- The exercise specifies that **user_a** and **user_b** must have the possibility to edit the common file **/home/share/test**.

For this you have to establish proper permissions for the common directory as also for the aforementioned file in the common directory.

chmod -R 770 /home/share

- Check your work by typing
ls -l /home

The output of the **list (ls -l)** command will show referring to the **/home/share** directory something like this :

```
drwxrwx--x  2  nobody  shared_group  4096  Apr  1  12:00  share
```

This output indicates that **share** is a directory (**d**) created at **12:00** on **April the 1st**, has **4096K** in size, belongs to the group named **shared_group**, owned by **nobody** and in this directory the owner has read-write-execute (**rwx**) permission, the group has read-write-execute (**rwx**) permission and others have only execute (**--x**) permission.

- Open with a text editor the **/etc/fstab** file and edit it by adding **acl** on the line referring to **/home** directory. Supposing that your **/home** directory is mounted already on **/dev/sda3** device (remember the **df -h** command !), then the aforementioned line should look like this :

```
LABEL=/home    /home    ext3    defaults,acl    1 2
```

- Remount **/home** directory reflecting the changes

  mount -o remount -o acl /dev/sda3 /home

  or

  mount -o remount -o acl /home

- Use the **getfacl /home/share** command to see what are the default ACL settings for the aforementioned directory:

```
[root@localhost ~]# getfacl /home/share/
getfacl: Removing leading '/' from absolute path names
# file: home/share
# owner: nobody
# group: shared_group
user::rwx
group::rwx
other::---
```

- Use the **setfacl** command to establish the proper **ACL** settings for the common directory you've created:

  setfacl -m u:user_a:rwx /home/share
  setfacl -m u:user_b:rwx /home/share
  setfacl -m u:user_c:r-x /home/share
  setfacl -m mask:rwx /home/share

- Check again with **getfacl /home/share.**
  Now it should show:

```
[root@localhost ~]# getfacl /home/share/
getfacl: Removing leading '/' from absolute path names
# file: home/share
# owner: nobody
# group: shared_group
user::rwx
user:user_a:rwx
user:user_b:rwx
user:user_c:r-x
group::rwx
mask::rwx
other::---
```

But this is not enough. According to the requirements of the exercise **user_c** must have some limitations regarding the **/home/share/test** file. This is done by establishing **ACL** settings also for this file:

> **setfacl -m u:user_a:rwx /home/share/test**
> **setfacl -m u:user_b:rwx /home/share/test**
> **setfacl -m u:user_c:r- - /home/share/test**
> **setfacl -m mask:rwx /home/share**

Check your work by using again the **getfacl** command:

```
[root@localhost ~]# getfacl /home/share/test
getfacl: Removing leading '/' from absolute path names
# file: home/share/test
# owner: nobody
# group: shared_group
user::rwx
user:user_a:rwx
user:user_b:rwx
user:user_c:r--
group::rwx
mask::rwx
other::---
```

- Login as **user_a** and modify the **/home/share/test** file. Add some text in it save your work and logout.

- Login as **user_b** and modify the **/home/share/tes**t. Add some new lines, save it and logout.
- Login as **user_c** and try to access the **/home/share/test** file.

You've noticed that as long as you login as **user_a** or **user_b**, you can access **/home/share** directory, you can create, modify or even delete files in this directory regardless which user created the files.

But once logged in as **user_c** you should be able only to read the content of the shared directory but not creating or modify any files in it.

You can go further extending the requirements of the exercise and by using the special permissions SGID and sticky bit, any file created in the shared directory to have group ownership established to **shared_group**:

>   **chmod -R 3770 /home/share**

Setup disk quota for users

Setting up disk quotas is necessary to prevent users and groups to consume all disk space.

There are two methods to configure disk quotas for users (eventually for groups): by the number of files a user is allowed to create (inodes) or by effective space on disk a user is allowed to occupy (blocks measured in kilobytes).

There are a few easy steps to configure disk quotas considering the effective space on disk a user is allowed to use :

- First make sure that **quota-[version_number].rpm** package is installed:

>   **rpm -qa | grep quota**

If the package is installed you'll have a response similar to **quota-[version_number].el[n]**, where **[version_number]** = the number of the default or updated version of the package and **el[n]** = Enterprise Linux n (Example: **el5**)

- The next step is to verify if the kernel has quota enabled:

>   **cat /boot/config-[kernel_version_number].el[n] | grep QUOTA**

In the expression above **[kernel_version_number]** represent the number of the kernel default or updated number.

If the returned answer will contain any of this: CONFIG_QUOTA=y and/or CONFIG_QUOTACTL=y, then kernel has quota enabled.

The entry CONFIG_QUOTA=y indicates that limits on usage are enabled while the CONFIG_QUOTACTL=y entry indicates that disk quota manipulation is enabled.

- Supposing that **/home** is the directory you want to enable quota on, backup first your **/etc/fstab** file before opening and modifying it with a text editor and introduce **usrquota** if you want to establish only quota for users, or **grpquota** if you want to establish quota for groups or both if you want to establish quota for users and groups, too.
  In this example I have added only quota for users so after editing, your **/etc/fstab** should look similar to this :

```
LABEL=/home        /home  ext3      defaults,usrquota 1          2
```

Observations
*I remind you once again to backup your **/etc/fstab** file before doing any modifications in it.*

When you modify this file be sure that the column you're editing will contain no spaces between the comma(s) and words and also the edited line will not wrap to the next line.
*Remember the earlier discussion about the **/etc/fstab** file.*
Be sure you'll have six distinctive columns on the edited line.

*If you want to add also quota for groups then the line referring to **/home** directory would look like this **in /etc/fstab** :*

```
LABEL=/home   /home   ext3  defaults,usrquota,grpquota    1    2
```

- Remount **/home** with the new settings:
  mount -o remount /home

- Create quota files.
  Use **quotacheck** command to create these files in **/home** directory. For my example I'll use the aforementioned command to create the

/home/aquota.user file because I have added only user quota for the **/home** directory.

quotacheck -cum /home

In case you added also quota for groups, to create the similar file **/home/aquota.group** but referring to groups, the command must be typed included also the **-g** operator:

quotacheck -cugm /home

- Edit **aquota.user** file by typing from a terminal:

edquota -u user_a

The command will open in **vi** editor the **aquota.user** file and it'll display something similar to this:

```
Disk quotas for user user_a (uid 500):
Filesystem        blocks      soft      hard      inodes      soft      hard
/dev/sdb1            32          0         0          8          0         0
```

To set the amount of space **user_a** is allowed to use, you need to edit only the section referring to the soft limit.
Assuming that you'll want **user_a** to use only 256MB of space on **/home**, you have to edit the file like this:

```
Disk quotas for user user_a (uid 500):
Filesystem        blocks      soft      hard      inodes      soft      hard
/dev/sdb1            32        256000      0          8          0         0
```

- Save your settings in this file and then check quota:

repquota -a

At this point **user_a** is allowed to use 256MB of space on **/home** directory. He can still go over this limit for a period of 7 days established by default. After 7 days, files totalizing an amount that passes the 256MB limit will remain in **/home/user_a** directory but **user_a** won't be able to create any more files.

If you're a system administrator, proceeding like this, **user_a** won't know about this 7 days grace period.

A nice way to warn him that he passed over his quota is by editing also
the **hard limit** section establishing a certain grace period of time that
user_a will have until he must get again under the 256MB limit already
established.

The hard limit represents the absolute limit an user is allowed to use. In this
case you'll have also to set up a grace period.
Supposing that you establish a 300MB for the **hard limit**, your **aquota.user**
file will look like this:

```
Disk quotas for user user_a (uid 500):
Filesystem      blocks     soft      hard     inodes      soft      hard
/dev/sdb1          32     256000    300000      8          0         0
```

- When both **soft** and **hard** limit are set, you need to specify a grace
  period by using the following command:

  edquota -t

This command will open in **vi** editor the file referring to the grace period:

```
Grace period before enforcing soft limits for users:
Time units may be: days, hours, minutes, or seconds
      Filesystem     Block grace period     Inode grace period
      /dev/sdb1              7days                  7days
```

As you can see this file reflects the default 7 days grace period of time.
You can edit both sections here (block and inode grace period) using
whatever you want to establish as grace period: a certain number of days,
hours or, seconds.
Just be sure no spaces interfere between numbers and words.

Examples:

> **7days**
> **10minutes**
> **3seconds**

At this point, considering that 7 days were chosen as grace period, **user_a**
can create files in **/home/user_a** directory even if these files exceed 256MB.
When this will happen, he is still allowed to create files occupying up to
300MB (in this example he can use practically an addition of 44 MB) but he

will be notified about disk quota exceeded. In this case he'll have seven days to get back again under 256MB.

- Practice using the **dd** command to create files having 256MB or more. It's the best way to verify your work.
  Login as **user_a** and type:

dd if=/dev/zero of=file_name bs=1k count=256000

In this expression **file_name** is the name of the file you want to create having 256MB (256000KB)

- If you have other users on your system that you'd want to modify quota after the existing **user_a**'s quota use the same **edquota** command including the **-p** operator:

edquota -up user_a user_b user_c

Other said, the already existing users named **user_b** and **user_c** will have the same settings, regarding quota, as **user_a**.

You'll have to follow similar steps when you wish to prevent a group to consume too much disk space only that this time you'll have to edit **/etc/fstab** as I have shown you introducing **grpquota.**

To create the **/home/aquota.group** file you'll need to use the **quotacheck -cgm /home** command while for editing the soft and/or hard limit, the used command will be **edquota -g group_name** where **group_name** is the name of the group you want to modify quota for.

As for establishing quota for different existing groups after an already setup group quota the command will be **edquota -gp main_group group_a group_b** where **main_ group** is the name of the group with an already setup quota, **group_a** and **group_b** are the names of the groups that will have same settings regarding quota as for **main_group.**

Observations
*Users can check their quotas without seeing quotas for other users by typing from a terminal the **quota** command.*

Having the possibility to establish same quota for different users/groups after it was already setup for one user/group is extremely helpful.

*Imagine you have to setup a mail server with thousands of clients. In this case it's almost impossible to use **edquota** command for each and every user or group you want to setup quota for.*
*Consider the use of the -p operator included in **edquota** command along with -u or -g more than time savers.*

Quotas for users and/or groups can be setup also by inods.
In my example, you can see that section referring to **inods** indicates number eight (**8**), zero (**0**) for soft limit and also zero (**0**) for hard limit.

You can conclude that **user_a** has already **8** files in he's home directory according to the fact that in Linux® one inod number correspounds to one file.

Using the same commands and following the same steps you can setup quota for users or groups limiting the number of files a user or a group is allowed to create.

Exercise
Setup quota on **/home** directory so **user_a** will be able to add one single 512MB file in his home directory.

- First check the existence of **quota-[version_number].rpm** package.

- Check if kernel has quota enabled.

- Assuming that there's enough disk space left in **/home** directory to perform this exercise, you'll have to edit the **/etc/fstab** file and add **usrquota** on the appropriate line.

- Next step is to remount **/home** directory with the new settings:

  mount -o remount /home

- Create **aquota.user** file by typing from a terminal:

  quotacheck -cum /home

- Edit quota for **user_a**

  edquota -u user_a

You'll have to add the 512MB value correspounding to the **soft limit** and also to the **hard limit** in the **blocks** section. This way you'll establish first the size of the file according to the requirements of this exercise.

The exercise requires also that **user_a** is allowed to create only one more file. For this, observe the number displayed under **inodes** section.

To whatever number you'll see there, add **1** obtaining the value you'll have to introduce under soft and hard limit in this section.

Example :

> If under `inodes` you'll see the value 8 then the value you'll have to introduce under `soft` and under `hard` (both referring to the inodes section!) should be `9` where **9** represents **8** files already existing plus **1** more.

- Establish the **block grace** period and **inod grace** period:

edquota -t

In the file that opens you'll have to add under **Block grace period** and **Inod grace period** the same value representing the maximum number of days, minutes, seconds that will be the granted grace period.

For this exercise add for example one second (written **1seconds**) under both sections:

```
         Block grace period              Inod grace period
              1seconds                        1seconds
```

I have chosen such as short grace period so the results will take place immediately.

- Save your work and verify your settings:

repquota -a

- Login as **user_a** and verify his quota by typing from a terminal:

quota

- Use the **dd** command to create a 512MB file named **test_file:**

  dd if=/dev/zero of=test_file bs=1k count=512000

- Try to create another file now by typing **touch file1** and see what happens.

Pluggable Authentication Modules - PAM

PAM is a system based on dynamically loadable library modules created to manage the users authentication process in Linux® having the libraries located in the **/lib/security** directory.

Any application controlled by PAM has a configuration file in **/etc/pam.d** directory.
A closer look to these configuration files reveals the mechanism through which PAM controls the authentication process.

First you'll notice that all lines in any PAM configuration file have the same structure:

```
module_type     control_flag     module_path     arguments
```

PAM system uses four different types of modules: **authentication (auth)**, **account, password** and **session**.

auth	- establishes user's identity usually asking for a password and checking it.
account	- grants or denies access based on availability of accounts, passwords or time period when users are allowed to log in.
password	- controls password policies
session	- manages the user's session after user was authenticated on the system

A **control_flag** has to be associated to a **module_type** so **PAM** system will know what to do in case the module works or not.

There are five types of control_flags defined by PAM system:

required	- when a required module is checked successfully the command proceeds.

	- if a required module fails the user won't be notified until all modules of the same type are tested.
requisite	- if the module fails the process is stopped and user is notified immediately.
sufficient	- if the module is checked successfully the user is authenticated to the service.
optional	- the module result is ignored regardless of success or failure.
include	- this flag includes all directives contained in the respective configuration file regarding **module_type.**

The **module_path** indicates the path and filename of the PAM library used to control the respective function.
Arguments are optional and they can be specified for each module.
For example, let's consider this entry:

```
auth required pam_listfile.so onerr=succeed item=user
sense=deny file=/etc/user.deny
```

If this entry is added to any configuration file in **/etc/pam.d**, the result will be that any user specified in **user.deny** file won't have access to the tool associated with the respective configuration file you have added this entry for. So you'll have to create the **/etc/user.deny** file and add in it the user names you want to have access denied to that particular tool.

If you want users to have access denied to a terminal, you have to create the **/etc/nologin** file.
Add in it this text for example: ACCESS DENIED

Try to login from a terminal as a non privileged user.
The message will flash fast and you won't be able to login.
If you'll try to login using GUI, the message from **/etc/nologin** file appears with the same result.
Login as root from a terminal and this time you'll see the message **ACCESS DENIED** but access will be granted.
This is possible because once created the **/etc/nologin** file, PAM system is instructed through it's **/etc/pam.d/nologin** configuration file to take action accordingly.

Chapter 4. Package management

To install or remove software, upgrading existing software, patching system's kernel, Red Hat® Enterprise Linux® based distributions use RPM – The Red Hat Package Manager tool.

An RPM package is in fact a container that includes binary installation scripts and documentation files for a specific application.

If previously, for defining the **quota** package I have used the expression **quota-[version_number].rpm,** now I can explain what the simplified expression **[version_number]** means.

For example, my installation media referring to the quota package contains an expression like this:

> **quota-3.13-1.2.3.2.el5.i386.rpm**

quota	- the name of the software contained by the RPM package.
3.13	- the version number of the quota software.
1.2.3.2.el5	- package release (number of times the package was rebuilt using the same software version) specifying also the distribution it was intended for. In this case el5 (Enterprise Linux 5).
i386	- the architecture the package was built for. In this case Intel 32-bit architecture.

To install an RPM package you'll use the **rpm** command with the **-i** operator.

> **rpm -i package_name.rpm**

When installing a package I prefer to use also the **-v** and **-h** operators associated with this command so I'll have a better view over the installation progress.

rpm -ivh package_name.rpm

I suggest to use **man rpm** command to see all options associated with this command.

Upgrading a package is done if you'll use the following commands:

rpm -Uvh package_name.rpm
or
rpm -Fvh package_name.rpm

Note again the use of **-v** and **-h** operators along with:
-   **-U**   - used for upgrading any existing package. If there is no previously installed version of the specified package it will install the desired package.
-   **-F**   - used for upgrading only the existing package. If the package wasn't installed previously no other action is taken.

To remove an RPM package the use of command will be :

rpm -e package_name

Installing, upgrading or removing any package is done according to some required or not dependencies.
For example, a package won't be installed if dependencies are required. Installation will fail and you'll see an error message indicating that some dependencies are missing.

The **--force** option will solve this problem by ignoring the dependencies and force installing the package, but this is not recommended because other problems may occur.

You can use the **rpm** command to install a package located at a certain URL. For example if you have an active Internet connection and you want to install the package named **package_name.rpm** located at **ftp://ftp.database.net/pub/package_name.rpm** the use of the command will be:

rpm -ivh ftp://ftp.database.net/pub/package_name.rpm

If the desired package is located at an URL that demands an user name and a password to access it and assuming that you are able to provide this information, then the command will be issued under this form:

rpm -ivh ftp://user_name:password@ftp.database.net/pub/package_name.rpm

where **user_name** and **password** refers to the name and the password you'll have to introduce in order to gain access to that desired URL.

You have noticed that in previous chapters I've used the **rpm** command associated with **-q** and **-a** operators in this form:

rpm --qa | grep package_name

This way of using the **rpm** command queries (**-q**) all packages (**-a**) in order to find the desired (if installed) **package_name.**
If the searched **package_name** is not found, the command won't return any answer.

If you want to verify the signature of an RPM package you can use either **md5sum** command or **rpm --checksig** command.

Usually when you download an RPM package from a data base located on a mirror, a text file containing the MD5 checksum is also provided along with the package.
To check the package signature you'll have to type from a terminal, the following command:

md5sum package_name.rpm

The output of this command is a value that you'll have to compare with the value you have found on the provided text file.
If the values are the same then the package is trustful.

If you want to check the signature of a certain RPM package located on your DVD containing your Red Hat® Enterprise Linux® based distribution you'll need to mount your DVD into **/media** directory and first import the GPG key provided by your DVD.

Assuming that your Linux distribution is CentOS, from a terminal type:

rpm --import /media/CentOS_5.3_Final/RPM-GPG-KEY-Centos-5

Once imported the GPG key you can check the integrity of any RPM package on your installation media by typing :

rpm --checksig /media/CentOS_5.3_Final/CentOS/package_name.rpm

Sometimes you'll need additional software for your Linux® distribution. Downloading and then installing the correspounding RPM packages containing the desired software might not be quite easy just using the **rpm -ivh** command because some dependencies are needed.

This problem was solved once YUM (The Yellowdog Updater Modified) was incorporated in all Red Hat® Enterprise Linux® 5 based distributions.

If you have an active Internet connection, a simple command like **yum install package_name** typed from a terminal will connect your computer to the default repositories listed in the **/etc/yum.repos.d** directory of your Linux® distribution downloading and installing the desired package with all necessary dependencies.

The same result will be obtained if you prefer to use a graphical tool called the **Package Manager (Pirut)** by typing from a terminal **pirut** or go to **Applications**, choose **Add/Remove Software**, introduce the password for **root** when asked and browse, search or list all desired packages.

The **yum** command comes with a lot of options (install, remove, update, check-update, etc) so don't forget to consult the man pages (**man yum**) to get all necessary explanations.
If you want to update your system, all you have to do is to open a terminal, login as root and type :

yum update

All default repositories will be queried for updates and if any update is found it will be installed with all dependencies.

If you prefer the graphical tool **Red Hat Package Updater** (**Pup**), type **pup** from a terminal or go to **Applications**, select **System Tools** then click on **Software Updater** and introduce the password for **root** when asked.
The system will display all updates if any available.

What is a repository?

A repository is a file containing information about a certain database
that hosts a large number of RPM packages designed for a certain Linux
distribution.
The Red Hat® Enterprise Linux® based distributions hold these kind of files
in **/etc/yum.repos.d** directory.

The files located in the **/etc/yum.repos.d** directory are named in this manner:

repository_name.repo

When **yum** command (with different options) is summoned, scripts that
control YUM are instructed to search any database specified in those files
included in **/etc/yum.repos.d** directory.

For example, the file **rpmforge.repo** in my **/etc/yum.repos.d** directory
contains the following in formation:

```
# Name: RPMforge RPM Repository for Red Hat Enterprise 5 - dag
# URL: http://rpmforge.net/
[rpmforge]
name = Red Hat Enterprise $releasever - RPMforge.net - dag
#baseurl = http://apt.sw.be/redhat/el5/en/$basearch/dag
mirrorlist = http://apt.sw.be/redhat/el5/en/mirrors-rpmforge
#mirrorlist = file:///etc/yum.repos.d/mirrors-rpmforge
enabled = 1
protect = 1
gpgkey = file:///etc/pki/rpm-gpg/RPM-GPG-KEY-rpmforge-dag
gpgcheck = 1
priority=2
```

The entry `enabled = 1` indicates that the repository is enabled. Disabling
any repository is done if you modify this entry to `enabled = 0`.

The entry `gpgcheck = 1` instructs **yum** to check the signature of the RPM packages.
You can see that the path to the location of the GPG key is also specified.
As you've noticed, there are some additional entries (**protect** and **priorities**)
in this file.
These entries refer to specific plugins that are recommended to be used
especially if you'll configure your system to look also for third party
repositories.

In order to use any of the following plugins for **yum**, first you'll have to check if plugins are enabled in the **/etc/yum.conf** file.

Look for an entry like `plugins = 1`.
It should be enabled by default in all Red Hat® Enterprise Linux® 5 based distributions.

The fastestmirror plugin

If the file that defines a repository contains an entry that points to multiple mirrors, this plugin will establish a connection to each specified mirror and after timing the connection will make a chart of these mirrors according to the time factor. So the fastest mirror will be at the top of this chart and the slowest will be at the bottom.
When you'll use **yum** to install the desired package, if this plugin is enabled, you'll download and install the package from the fastest mirror.

- Download and install this plugin:

  yum install yum-fastestmirror

- Be sure that the plugin is enabled.
  Use the **cat** command to find if the **/etc/yum/pluginconf.d/ fastestmirror.conf** file contains the entry `enabled = 1`

  cat /etc/yum/pluginconf.d/fastestmirror.conf

The protectbase plugin

This plugin will protect the repository that contains the entry `protect = 1` against updates from other repositories.
It is recommended to be used if you want to install additional software located on third party repositories other than the default repositories for your Linux® distribution.
In these conditions, if the plugin is not enabled, additional repositories may update certain system files unwanted to be modified in your system.

- Download and install this plugin

  yum install yum-protectbase

- Be sure that the plugin is enabled.
  Use the **cat** command to find if the **/etc/yum/pluginconf.d/protectbase.conf** file contains the entry enabled = 1

  cat /etc/yum/pluginconf.d/protectbase.conf

  - Edit all **.repo** files in **/etc/yum.repos.d** directory by adding protect = 1 for repositories you want to protect and protect = 0 for repositories you want unprotected.

Observation
*You should use ONLY ONE of these two plugins: **protectbase** or **priorities**. Once applied to repositories, these plugins act almost in the same manner.*

The priorities plugin

This plugin associates a number representing priority to a repository enforcing the desired protection of the repository.

- Download and install this plugin:

  yum install yum-priorities

- Be sure that the plugin is enabled.
  Use the **cat** command to find if the **/etc/yum/pluginconf.d/priorities.conf** file contains the entry enabled = 1

  cat /etc/yum/pluginconf.d/priorities.conf

If you'll use this plugin then you have to edit all **.repo** files in **/etc/yum.repos.d** by adding a line containing priority = n, where n = { 1, 2, ..., 99 } is the number that defines the priority for that repository.

The value **n = 1** will establish the highest priority for the repository while the value **n = 99** indicates the lowest priority so, the repository with the lower priority won't be able to update the repository with a higher priority.

The rpm -ivh new_kernel command vs. the rpm -Uvh new_kernel command

Usually an updated kernel contains new features and fixed security issues that helps your Linux® distribution to be more secure and run better.
However, a new kernel may create problems especially when you also install updated software for your hardware.
Using the **rpm -ivh new_kernel** command to upgrade to a new kernel or, if you have an active Internet connection, using **yum install kernel** you'll obtain the same result: a new kernel will be installed maintaining also the old kernel version on your system.

This is extremely useful in case something goes wrong while managing the software dedicated for you computer's hardware.

For example you want to use a web camera but you know that the associated drivers for the desired web camera are contained in the newest released kernel for your Linux® distribution.

You'll use the **rpm -ivh new_kernel** or **yum install kernel** command and after restarting your system with the new kernel, you'll be able to use your web cam.
Then you'll open a few web pages and suddenly the image on your monitor is scrambled and your computer freezes.

You reboot the computer, this time with the old kernel and after running the **dmesg** command you'll find that the video drivers caused the problem when you used the new kernel version.
In this case, to solve your web cam problem, it is better to compile the old kernel selecting the appropriate video options (if provided) for your web cam.

Considering the same example, if you have used the **rpm -Uvh new_kernel**, your old kernel would have been overwritten!
If things would have happened as I have described previously, you'd spent a lot of time rebooting your system with a rescue disk and using the **linux rescue** command trying to reinstall the existing kernel.

For the future, remember to keep in your system also the old stable kernel version along with the newest version to prevent any unpleasant situation.
Even if your new kernel works very good on your system, do not hurry up to remove your old kernel!

Chapter 5.   Basic system configuration tools

Network Configuration

Based on the TCP/IP protocol, there are two ways you can configure a network interface regarding the IP address allocation point of view: **static** configured network interface and **dynamic** configured network interface. For a static configured interface, the IP address always remains the same.

Servers use a static IP address so even after a reboot they will maintain the same IP address making possible the access of a potential client computer.

A dynamic configured interface has an IP address that changes every time when you're connecting to a network.
In other words, each time you login into your system, you'll have a different IP address allocated by a DHCP server configured by your Internet Service Provider (ISP) or by yourself as you'll learn in an upcoming chapter.

Red Hat® Enterprise Linux® 5 based distributions hold and retrieve networking information in the **/etc/sysconfig/network-scripts** directory. Along many files contained in this directory you'll find the **ifcfg-ethN** script that indicates the way your network interface is configured.

The following tables present examples describing static and dynamic configured network interfaces.

Table 7

Static Configuration	Description
DEVICE=ethN	Specifies the device for which the settings are referred to. N={0,1,2,....n}
HWADDR=00:02:5C:41:57:A6	The MAC address associated with the specified device
IPADDR=192.168.100.123	Specified static IP address
NETMASK=255.255.255.0	Netmask associated with the static IP address
GATEWAY=192.168.100.1	The IP address of the system or device used by your computer to establish connections with other networks
ONBOOT=yes	The device is brought up when system boots. Options are yes or no.
Type=Ethernet	Specifies the type of network interface used. In this case it's a wired connection. For a wireless connection the entry is Type=Wireless
USERCTL=no	Optional inserted, this entry establishes if regular users are entitled to bring the device up or down using options like yes or no.

Table 8

Static Configuration	Description
`DEVICE=ethN`	Specifies the device for which the settings are referred to. N={0,1,2,....n}
`HWADDR=00:02:5C:41:57:A6`	The MAC address associated with the specified device
`BOOTPROTO=dhcp`	Indicates that your computer retrieves the IP from a DHCP server if specified this way.
`ONBOOT=yes`	The device is brought up when system boots. Options are `yes` or `no`.
`Type=Ethernet`	Specifies the type of network interface used. In this case it's a wired connection. For a wireless connection the entry is `Type=Wireless`
`USERCTL=no`	Optional inserted, this entry establishes if regular users are entitled to bring the device up or down using options like `yes` or `no`.

If you need to see your network settings for a certain network device attached to your computer you can type from a terminal one of the following commands:

ifconfig ethN
　　　　or
cat /etc/sysconfig/network-scripts/ifcfg-ethN

If your computer has only one network card, for sure the device will be detected as **eth0** so replace **N** accordingly.

The global network settings are in the **/etc/sysconfig/network** file. Issuing the **cat /etc/sysconfig/network** command, depending of your configuration, you'll see something similar to this:

Table 9

Setting	Description
NETWORKING=yes	Normally set to yes, indicates that networking is enabled.Other option is no
NETWORKING_IPV6=no	If IPV6 support is enabled, this entry can be set also with yes or no options.
HOSTNAME=localhost.localdomain	The DNS that resolves your network. If this entry is not defined, your computer will ask DNS for a name to associate with. If DNS doesn't have a name the computer will use the default name localhost.localdomain If your computer retrieves networking information from a DHCP server, you can define this or not.
GATEWAY=192.168.100.1	Specifies the IP address of the system or device used by your computer to establish connections with other networks. This entry can be specified here or in **/etc/sysconfig/network-scripts/ ifcfg-ethN** file. If your network settings are obtained from a DHCP server, this entry is not necessary.

To find your HOSTNAME you can type from a terminal the **hostname** command. Also using a terminal you can change your HOSTNAME by typing:

hostname new_host.new_domain

I've considered that **new_host** is the new name you want to assign for your host and **new_domain** is the new domain name.

Example: **hostname mycomputer.home**

After you have used the **hostname** command to change the HOSTNAME, you'll have to edit also the **/etc/sysconfig/network** file introducing the correspounding value you have chosen, so next time you'll reboot your computer, the desired settings for HOSTNAME will remain.

What is DNS?

DNS (Domain Name Service) is a service that translates host names into network addresses and vice-versa.
Every time you type in your Internet Browser something like **www.my_example.com**, your computer asks the local DNS server what IP address is assigned for **my_example.com**

The DNS settings used by your computer are in the **/etc/resolv.conf** file. You can see the content of this file if from a terminal type:

> **cat /etc/resolv.conf**

In this file you'll see two directives: `search` and `nameserver`

The `search` directive specifies domains that should be tried when an incomplete DNS name is given to a command.
The `nameserver` directive is the most important one because specifies the IP address of one or more DNS servers your computer should use.

Another important file is the **/etc/hosts** file.
This file contains IP addresses for systems on your network.
By default, this file contains an entry like this :

```
127.0.0.1     localhost.localdomain     localhost
```

I remind you that **127.0.0.1** is the loopback interface. This represents the internal IP address of your computer.

Let's say you have created a web server on your computer.
If you type **http://localhost** or **http://127.0.0.1** into your Internet Browser you'll see the Apache test page which indicates that the HTTP server you just configure is up and running on your computer.

Observation

There are three IP addresses designated for your computer:

127.0.0.1   — *loopback interface which says that localhost is 127.0.0.1 and vice-versa.*

192.168.1.100 *(for example!)*   — *the IP address that your computer uses to connect to different computers in your LAN.*

*For a home computer, usually, this is retrieved from a DHCP server so it might not be the same next time you'll reboot your computer. Check it with the **ifconfig** command.*

77.77.77.100 *(for example!)*   — *the IP address your computer uses to connect to computers on other networks.*
This is your, so called, external IP address.

The router designated for your LAN uses this IP address to permit the exchange of information between users included in your LAN and the Internet. All computers in this LAN will use the same Gateway (according to my example above, 192.168.1.1) to gain access to this unique router's IP address.

The procedure of allocating one single external IP address to many computers on a specific LAN is called IP Masquerading.
I'll present this procedure later in this book.

For diagnosing and modifying network settings, several commands are used with different options.

To bring a specific network interface up or down you can use **ifup** / **ifdown** commands

ifup eth0   – will bring up the **eth0** network interface

ifdown eth0   – will bring down the **eth0** network interface

Probably the most used command is the **ifconfig** command.
With this command you can display and also configure settings for a certain network interface

ifconfig — typed from a terminal without any specifications will display network settings for all your network adapters including the loopback interface (**lo**) as in the following example:

`Link encap : Ethernet` — indicates that the network adapter is a wired (Ethernet) network card

`HWaddr 00:02:5C:41:57:A6` — the MAC address of the network adapter

`inet addr : 192.168.48.100` — the IP address designated to this computer by a DHCP server

`Bcast : 192.168.49.255` — the broadcast address indicating the specific subnet this computer is part of

`Mask : 255.255.255.0` — the subnet mask assigned for the specified IP address

If you want to find the network settings for a certain device then type:

ifconfig ethN — where **N** is the number of the network device you want the settings to be displayed for.

The **ifconfig** command also helps you assign a new IP address to a specific network adapter.
For example you want to change the IP address 192.168.48.100 and the netmask 255.255.255.0 and assign a new IP address 11.11.11.3 and a new netmask 255.255.0.0
From a terminal type:

ifconfig eth0 11.11.11.3 netmask 255.255.0.0

Type **ifconfig eth0** and notice the changes.
Same thing is obtain if you type:

> **ifconfig eth0 11.11.11.3/16**

Practice using **/24, /16, /8** and see how this modifies the subnet mask and the broadcast address.
My example refers just to the way you have to use this command in order to change the specified settings.
In real life this might not work with the broadcast address. So be sure to do the appropriate modifications.

Read the man pages for more information about this command (**man ifconfig**).

Another way to configure the network interface is by typing from a terminal the following command:

> **system-config-network-tui**

GUI also provides a tool to help you configure your network interface.
Select **System**, choose **Administration** and then **Network**.
The Network Configuration utility will display something like this :

All network interfaces will be displayed in this box.
To configure any of them, just select the desired one (in my example only
one is listed eth0) and then by pressing **Edit**, the next dialog box will give
you the possibility to configure it static or dynamic.
If you choose a static configuration for your network device, then don't
forget to press the DNS tab and insert there the correspounding IP address (or
addresses) for DNS.

A useful tool for checking your network activity is the **netstat** command.
If you associate the **-r** and **-n** operators to the **netstat** command the output
will display the kernel routing table (**-r** operator) and also the IP addresses
will be printed instead of trying to determine symbolic host (**-n** operator).
It is very useful when you want to avoid address lookups over the network.

```
[root@localhost ~]# netstat -rn
Kernel IP routing table
Destination Gateway  Genmask     Flags  MSS  Window  irtt  Iface
192.1.0.0   0.0.0.0  255.255.0.0  U     0    0       0     eth0
169.254.0.0 0.0.0.0  255.255.0.0  U     0    0       0     eth0
```

In my example you can see the output of the **netstat -rn** command organized
in eight columns.

Destination	- lists networks by IP address
Gateway	- lists gateway addresses. If no gateway is used, then an * will be displayed
Genmask	- lists the network mask.
Flags	- used to describe the route. This flags could be :

G = The route uses a gateway.
U = The interface used is up.
H = Only a single host can be reached through this route.
D = This route is dynamically created.
It will be displayed if the entry was created by an Internet Control Message Protocol(ICMP) redirect message.

M = Set if the table entry was modified by an ICMP redirect message.

MSS
- the Maximum Segment Size represents the size of the largest datagram the kernel will construct for transmission via this route.

Window
- represents the maximum amount of data the system will accept in a single burst from a remote host.

irtt
- Initial Round Trip Time. The TCP protocol counts how long it takes for the information to reach the target and back. According to this it will know how long it takes for the information to be retransmitted. Zero value indicates that the default is used.

Iface
- Refers to the interface used. In my example eth0.

Consult the man pages for more options regarding this command.
One more useful tool I'll present is the **arp** command. This command is associated with kernel's Address Resolution Protocol (ARP).
ARP is used to translate IP addresses to hardware interface addresses. With the **arp** command you can clear, add or dump kernel's ARP cache reflected in the **/proc/net/arp** file.
The out put of the arp command on my computer shows the following:

```
[root@localhost ~]# arp
Address          HWtype  HWaddress          Flags  Mask   Iface
192.168.49.2     ether   00:50:56:FB:48:1F  C             eth0
192.168.49.254   ether   00:50:56:FC:11:08  C             eth0
```

The information presented here is displayed on six columns. You can see how the known IP addresses in the first column are linked to hardware addresses in the third column.

The entries in the kernel's ARP cache can be marked with the following flags (column four) :

> c = complete
> M = permanent
> P = published

If the command detects duplicate IP addresses that can stop the network, then you can use the **arp** command with the **-d** operator to remove these unwanted computers:

arp -d example

The command issued as above will remove all ARP information about the computer named **example**.
If you want to add an entry in kernel's ARP cache then the command will be issued as follows:

arp -s example 00:02:5C:41:57:A6

where **00:02:5C:41:57:A6** is the hardware address (MAC address) of the computer named **example.**
More options that can be used with the **arp** command are listed in the man pages.

Printing with The Common Unix Printing System (CUPS)

If you have selected the Printing Support package group when your operating system was installed, for sure you have CUPS also installed.
There's no reason for panic if you forgot to do this.
You still can install CUPS with all necessary packages using either the Package Manager or, if from a terminal you'll type :

yum groupinstall printing

Check if the printing service is running with:

service cups status

If the service is installed but not running solve the problem with:

service cups start

Make sure next time when you'll reboot your computer, the service will start automatically:

chkconfig cups on

Now it's time to configure your printer.
There are two methods to do this from a GUI terminal:

- using The Printer Configuration Tool
- using the Web-based interface.

Configuring a printer with The Printer Configuration Tool

To start this tool you can type from a terminal **system-config-printer** or just go to **System**, choose **Administration**, then click on **Printing.**
Any method you'll choose to initiate this tool will display the following:

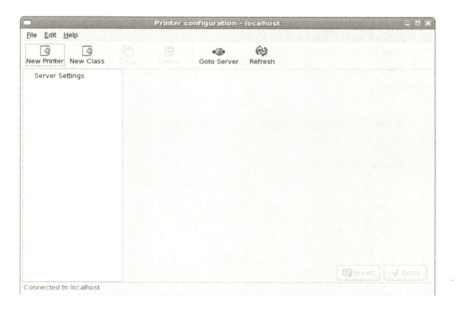

Click on the **New Printer** button:

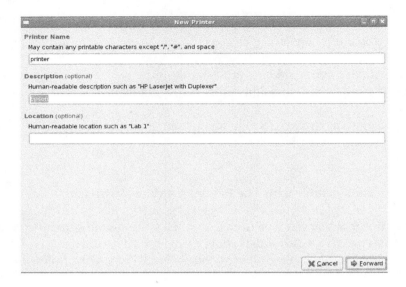

Select a printer name and a description.
In my example the printer is Epson.
Click **Forward** button after you finished introducing the requested
information.

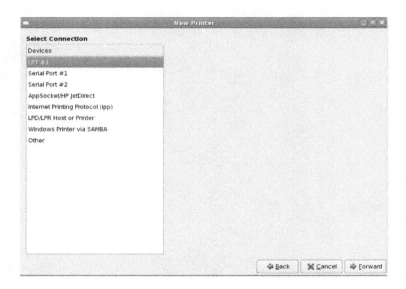

The new menu requires to select how your printer is connected to your computer. Choose the appropriate connection type and click **Forward**.

Then select the printer you want to add and click **Forward**.

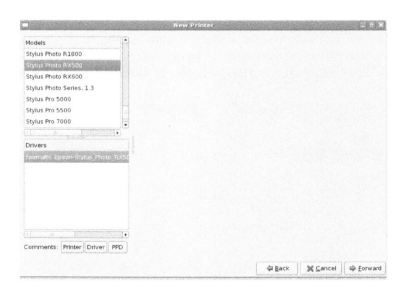

Choose the appropriate model if listed and click **Forward**.
The next screen shows that your printer was added (**Local Printer** section indicates this).

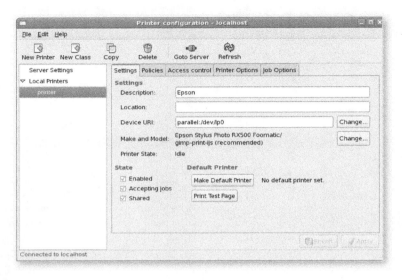

If you're practicing on a virtual machine, using the same method you can configure your computer to share a printer or to use a remote printer.

Supposing that you want to share a printer already configured on your computer, select from the main configuration window **Server Settings** then check the box **Share published printers connected to this system** as follows:

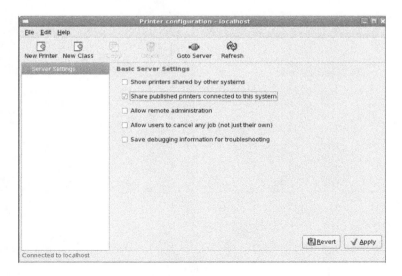

When you're done, click **Apply.**

If you power on a virtual machine and you start the Printer Configuration Tool on it, in the main menu select **Server Setting** but this time check the box **Show printers shared by other systems.**
Click **Apply** and close this menu so settings will take effect.
Open again the Printer Configuration tool on this new virtual machine and this time you should see a new section called **Remote Printers,** listing the printer you just shared previously as in the next figure:

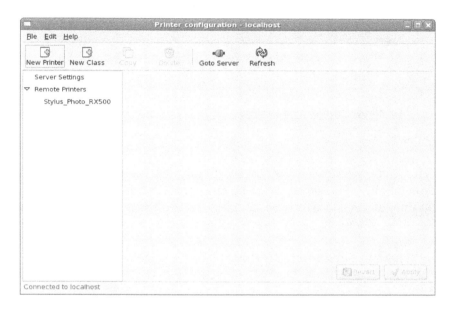

You can click on the printer's name listed here and in the menu that opens you'll notice some information regarding the remote printer.
To test if your remote printer is working, just click on Print Test Page button.

Configuring a printer using the Web-based interface

This method helps you configuring and sharing a printer by using your Internet Browser.
Open your Internet Browser and type in the address bar **http://localhost:631**

A web page will be opened displaying the following:

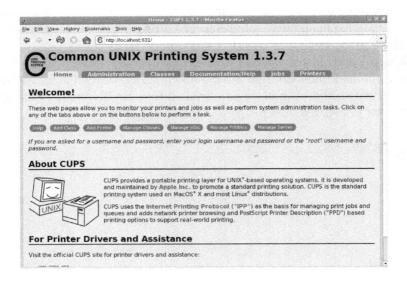

The Home tab contains a list of various options you can choose from according to how you want to manage one or more printers.
If you want to add a local printer, just click on **Add Printer** button and follow similar steps as for using the Printer Configuration Tool explained previously.

If you'll initialize the **Administration** tab the next menu will look like this:

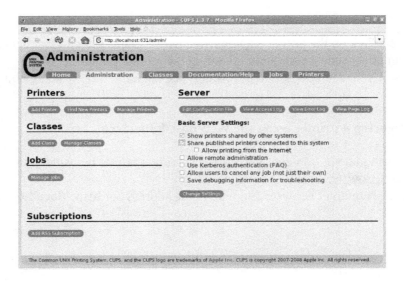

You can see in the **Basic Server Settings** that all you have to do to share, or see shared printers is checking the correspounding boxes with the specific indications.

All settings you might establish for your printer are reflected in the appropriate files contained in **/etc/cups** directory.

For example, the **/etc/cups/cupsd.conf** file which controls the CUPS server, shows several settings indicating also if the printer was correctly shared.

The information in this file is organized in containers similar to the Apache configuration file that I'll describe later in this book.

```
# Share local printers on the local network.
Browsing On
BrowseOrder allow,deny
BrowseAddress @LOCAL
DefaultAuthType Basic
<Location />
        Allow localhost
        # Allow shared printing...
        Order allow,deny
        Allow @LOCAL
</Location>
<Location /admin>
        Encryption Required
        Allow localhost6
        # Restrict access to the admin pages...
        Order allow,deny
</Location>
<Location /admin/conf>
        AuthType Basic
        Require user @SYSTEM
        Allow localhost
        # Restrict access to the configuration files...
        Order allow,deny
</Location>
```

The section `Share local printers on the local network`, through it's entries `Browsing On` and `BrowseAddress @LOCAL` indicates that the configured printer is shared on local network.

By changing the entry `BrowseAddress @LOCAL` into `BrowseAddress @ALL`, your printer won't be shared only with computers in the local LAN but with any computer from different connected networks.

The entries `DefaultAuthType Basic` and `AuthType Basic` refers to the fact that allowed users are authenticated based on directives in the **/etc/passwd** file.

The container `<Location /admin/conf>` as it is configured in my example, indicates that the remote access to the Web-based interface is supported only from the local network.
The only way to permit the other computers from different networks to remotely configure your printer in order to be able to use it, is to edit this section of the **/etc/cups/cupsd.conf** file by adding an entry that specifies the IP address or the domain names of those networks.

So the section **Restrict access to the configuration files...** in my example will look something like this :

```
Order allow,deny
Allow From 192.168.10.0/24
              or
Order allow,deny
Allow From 192.168.10.0/255.255.255.0
```

assuming that **192.168.10.0/24** is the network you want to allow remote access to the Web-based tool.

The Line Print Daemon (lpd) Commands

Printing a document it's not necessary to be done from a GUI interface. This also can be done by typing the right command from a terminal.
The **lpd** service provides some useful commands to handle printing jobs:

lpr (line print request) command	- allow users to send print requests to a local or remote printer
lpq (line print query) command	- shows printer queue status

lpc (line printer control) command	- if associated with **status** option will display all printers and queues. If no option is associated to this command then a prompt is displayed (**lpc>**)
lprm job_number command	- this command removes any unwanted job of the printer. To see all jobs in progress just type **lpq**

Examples:

lpr -# 2 /root/anaconda-ks.cfg	- will print two copies of the **/root/anaconda-ks.cfg** file
lpr -P Printer_Name root/anaconda-ks.cfg	- will print the file to the specified printer (in this case the printer name is **Printer_Name**)
lprm 78	- will remove the job number 78 from printing

Automating Linux tasks using cron and at

Cron and **at** are two utilities used to schedule a task to take place at a certain time. While **at** lets you specify one-time action to take place at a desired time, **cron** will do the job repeatedly.

Cron is configured to search for computer jobs in the **/etc/crontab** and /etc/cron.d directories as also will search for user jobs in the **/var/spool/cron** directory.

To schedule a job using **cron** you have to create a table with a certain format specifying time and date for the command or the script you want to be executed.

The format of such **crontab** looks like this:

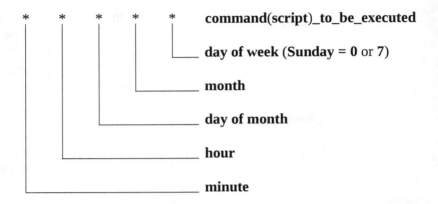

The **crontab -e** command will open in **vi** editor a **crontab** giving you the possibility to edit it as necessary.
Same command will edit an existing crontab.

crontab -r	– will remove a crontab
crontab –l	– lists entries in a crontab
crontab -u user_name	– gives **root** user the possibility to edit a user's crontab.

Examples:

Every 30 minutes on every Friday echo "Reminder" and mail it to user at example.net:

```
*/30 * * * 5 echo "Reminder" | mail user@example.net
```

Every day at 18:00 from Monday to Friday bring down the network device eth0:

```
0   18   *    *  1-5  /sbin/ifdown eth0
```

The **at** system is used to schedule jobs that run only one time.
For example, if you want to send a file to a user at 10:00, from a terminal type:

    at 10:00

A prompt will be displayed and you'll have to introduce the command here:

```
at>  cat /home/file | mail user@example.net
```

To initiate **at** after introducing the desired command, press the **Ctrl** and **D** keys

If you want to see the scheduled job just type **atq**.
To remove a job type **atrm job_number** where **job_number** will be the number of the job displayed when the **atq** command was issued.

Examples of supported entries for **at** command:

> **at 10:45**
> **at 10 :45 1/12/2009**
> **at now + 15 minutes**
> **at now + 3 hours**
> **at now + 2 days**
> **at now + 1 week**

You can deny certain users to have access to **cron** and **at** utilities.
The associated files to deny access to **cron** or **at** are :

> **/etc/cron.deny**
> **/etc/at.deny**

If you open any of these files with a text editor, you'll add one user name per line in order to deny access to these services for any user you want.

Managing and monitoring system logs

Keeping track of the activities running on your system is a very important thing for a system administrator.
Two important utilities are loaded at startup by default in Red Hat® Enterprise Linux® based distributions helping you track any activity taking place on your system: **klogd** and **syslogd.**

The **klogd** daemon logs kernel messages and **syslogd** daemon logs all other activities. These daemons generate log files that can help you detecting any activity taking place at a certain moment on your system, so you can block or allow it by properly editing the associated configuration files.

From a terminal type **klogd** and/or **syslogd** to check if these services are running
The output should be something like :

> **klogd: Already running**
> and/or
> **syslogd: Already running**

Both daemons are instructed to be activated by the **/etc/init.d/syslog** script
but their behavior is determined by the **/etc/syslog.conf** file.
In other words, the **/etc/syslog.conf** file tells the aforementioned daemons
what and how activities on your system should be logged.

My **/etc/syslog.conf** file looks like this:

```
# Log all kernel messages to the console.
# Logging much else clutters up the screen.
#kern.*                                 /dev/console
# Log anything (except mail) of level info or higher.
# Don't log private authentication messages!
*.info;mail.none;news.none;authpriv.none /var/log/messages

# The authpriv file has restricted access.
authpriv.*                             /var/log/secure

# Log all the mail messages in one place.
mail.*                                 /var/log/maillog

# Log cron stuff
cron.*                                 /var/log/cron

# Everybody gets emergency messages
*.emerg                                    *

# Save new errors of level crit and higher in a special file.
uucp,news.crit                         /var/log/spooler

# Save boot messages also to boot.log
local7.*                               /var/log/boot.log

news.=crit                       /var/log/news/news.crit
news.=err                        /var/log/news/news.err
news.notice                      /var/log/news/news.notice
```

Observation
*If you check your **/etc/syslog.conf** file it's possible that you won't see exactly
the same entries like in my example because you might not have installed*

in your computer same services as I did. So, in your case the associated directives are missing.

The entries in this file are all variations of a pretty clear pattern:

```
Item.Priority_level          path_to_the_specific_log_file
```

Item indicates the process or daemon translated specifically by using the terms presented in the following table:

Table 10

Item	Description
authpriv	User general and private authentication
cron	**cron** daemon messages
kern	Kernel messages
mail	Mail system messages
news	Usenet news messages
user	User processes
uucp	Messages regarding Unix-To-Unix-Copy-Program

Priority_level specifies the importance of the message translated into indicators presented in the following table:

Table 11

Priority Listed from highest to lowest	Description
emerg	Panic conditions that should be transmitted to all users
alert	Conditions that should be corrected immediately
crit	Warnings about critical conditions
err	Errors
warn	Warning messages
notice	Non-error conditions that might require special handling
info	Info messages that don't require special handling
debug	Messages used for debugging a program
none	Generic priority level that logs all messages at all levels

You have noticed the asterisk (*****) which specifies all **Items** or all **Priority_levels,** depending of the position you'll place it (after or before the dot).

Example:

```
Items.*  or  *.Priority_Level
```

Multiple **Items** could be specified for a single **Priority_Level** using a coma (**,**) and also multiple entries could be specified in a single action by using the semicolon (**;**)

Examples:

```
uucp,news.crit
```

```
*.info;mail.none;news.none;authpriv.none
```

Where are the log files ?

Most messages from **syslogd** daemon are files in the **/var/log/** directory.
Use the **ls** command to list the content of the **/var/log** directory.
Along the log files created by the **syslogd** daemon, you'll see here that other services like samba, squid, cups, http, etc have created their own log files.
In time the quantity of information in these files will increase making them very difficult to be read.
Fortunately, Red Hat® Enterprise Linux® based distributions come also with the logrotate utility.
This utility rotates log files according to the **/etc/logrotate.conf** file as also according to the configuration files in the **/etc/logrotate.d** directory. The cron daemon is responsible for running logrotate.

The content of the **/etc/logrotate.conf** file looks something like this:

```
# rotate log files weekly
weekly

# keep 4 weeks worth of backlogs
rotate 4
```

```
# create new (empty) log files after rotating old ones
create

#uncomment this is you want your log files compressed
#compress

# RPM packages drop log rotation information into this
directory
include /etc/logrotate.d

# no packages own wtmp - we'll rotate them here
/var/log/wtmp {
        monthly
        minsize 1M
        create 0664 root utmp
        rotate 1
}


# system-specific logs may be also be configured here.
```

Right from the beginning, this file indicates that log file rotation is done weekly and kept four weeks worth of previous log files. This also prevents uncontrolled expansion of the **/var/log** directory.

The next entry in this file creates a new empty file after the old files were rotated.
This is the reason why you see in the **/var/log/** directory multiple files with the same name containing different numbers at the end.
If you analyze the content of the **/etc/logrotate.d** directory you'll find out that the configuration files in this directory are referring to the rotation of the log files created by   other services I have mentioned.

A graphical tool called **System Log Viewer** is also available to help view, add or monitoring log files.
To initiate this tool you can type from a terminal **gnome-system-log** or go to **System**, choose **Administration** and then **System Log.**

After initiating this tool you can choose the desired log file from the left side of the panel while details about it will be displayed on the right side.

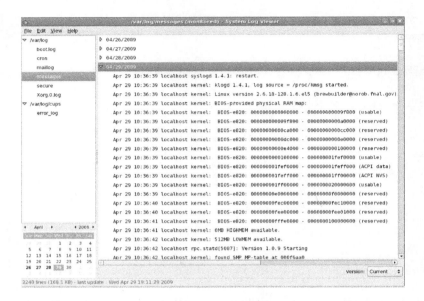

To add a new log file to be displayed in the left side of the panel, you have to choose **File** then **Open.**

The **Open Log** window appears and now you can select the log file you want to view as illustrated in the next image:

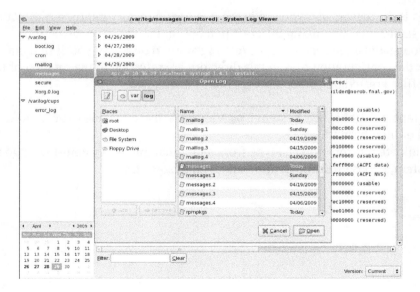

It really doesn't matter what method you'll choose to view log files as long as the preferred method leads you to a fast and accurate interpretation of the messages sent by your system when and if problems occurred.

Chapter 6.   The Web Server Package Group: Apache and Squid

The Apache Web Server

Apache is the most popular Web Server on the Internet.
It uses the regular HTTP protocol configured on **TCP port 80** and also the secure HTTPS protocol configured on **TCP port 80**.

You can install the needed packages for Apache server if from a terminal you type:

> **yum install httpd**

In case you'll want to configure Apache from GUI using the Apache Management tool you'll need a supplementary package installed:

> **yum install system-config-httpd**

If you want to install Apache and Squid with one single command then type :

> **yum groupinstall "Web Server"**

Basic Configuration

After you have installed the necessary packages check the status of the service and start it by issuing the following commands:

> **service httpd status**
> **service httpd start**

At this point, to verify if your Apache server is running you can either use your Internet browser or the **links** command from a terminal and type **http://localhost** or **http://127.0.0.1**.

You should see the default Apache Test Page indicating that the Apache server configured on local host is up and running.

If you want Apache to start every time you'll restart your computer then type the following command:

chkconfig httpd on

Apache server has it's configuration files in **/etc/httpd** directory and serves files, by default, from **/var/www/html** directory.
This service keeps it's log files in **/var/log/httpd** so if any problems occur you can consult the log files regarding the server or virtual hosts.

The default configuration file for the regular Apache server is **/etc/httpd/conf/httpd.conf** divided in three sections with detailed explanations. Take your time to analyze this file and read carefully the explanations provided for all directives.
More help you can find at **http://httpd.apache.org**

Before starting to configure your regular Apache server I strongly advise you to save first a copy of this file somewhere into your computer.
For example :

cp /etc/httpd/conf/httpd.conf /root

In case something goes wrong, all you have to do is to use the **cp** command again, this time to restore the file **httpd.conf** right at it's place in **/etc/httpd/conf** directory.

The overview of the **httpd.conf** file reveals, beside the multitude of the directives, also a certain way the information is structured in this file: the "containers".

Let's take for example this container:

```
#<Directory /home/*/pubic_html>
#       AllowOverride FileInfo AuthConfig Limit
#       Options MultiViews Indexes SymLinksIfOwnerMatch
IncludesNoExec
#       <Limit GET POST OPTIONS>
#               Order allow,deny
#               Allow from all
```

```
#        </Limit>
#        <LimitExcept GET POST OPTIONS>
#                Order deny,allow
#                Deny from all
#        </LimitExcept>
#</Directory>
```

It starts indicating the name of the item it refers to in between two brackets. In this case indicates a directory: **<Directory /home/*/public_html>**. Items could be also files, modules, locations, proxy or virtual host names.

It ends including the forward slash (/) followed by the name of the specified item.

If you want a certain container to be active, you need to remove the pound character # from in front of the lines that define the beginning and the end of the container as also from any line specifying settings inside of that container.

In this example the container is inactive because all lines start with the pound character # in front.

The directive **Include conf.d/*.conf** you'll also see in the **/etc/httpd/conf/httpd.conf** file indicates that files in the **/etc/httpd/conf.d** directory are included.

Simple Web Server Configuration

In what follows I'll present in a few steps a basic configuration for a simple Web Server.
I recommend the use of a Virtual Machine and configure it as a Web Server, then you can check your work either from your day by day system or from another Virtual Machine.
For the purpose of this exercise, disable **Firewall** and **SELinux**.

- From a terminal type **system-config-securitylevel** and check the **Disable** boxes for **Firewall** and **SELinux**. Then select **OK** to save your settings.

If you want to use the Security Level Configuration tool in GUI, go to **System**, choose **Administration** then click on **Security Level and Firewall**.

In the **Firewall Options** tab select **Firewall: Disabled.**
Then initiate the **SELinux** tab and select **SELinux Setting: Disabled**

- Open with your preferred text editor the **/etc/httpd/conf/httpd.conf** file.

I will modify and add specific entries in this file so they will reflect the following properties of this server:

a) Allow connections only from computers in the same LAN
  (host-based security)
b) Only certain users in the LAN will be able to connect to this
  server **(user-based security)**
c) Users will retrieve necessary information from the
  /var/www/html/example directory.

- The following line has to be uncommented (does not contain the pound character in front of it):

```
Listen 80
```

This means that communication through port 80 (established by default) is permitted so, in case you'll want Firewall activated, users will connect through this port to your Web Server.

- Find the line # Controls who can get stuff from this server. This section refers to host-based security
  By default it has two entries:

```
Order allow,deny
Allow from all
```

The first entry of this section written this way, indicates that all connections to your HTTP server are **denied** (Order allow, deny), while the second entry is the one you have to modify in order to allow connections only from your LAN (as specified in this exercise) :

```
Allow from 192.168.1.0/24
              or
Allow from 192.168.1.0/255.255.255.0
```

You have to replace the IP addresses I have used here as example with the IP address and the netmask specified for your own network.

Observation
If you want your server to accept connections from any computer with certain exceptions you can write these rules in this manner:

```
Order deny,allow
Deny from 192.168.100.33
```

In this case connections from any machine are accepted by default while connections coming from the machine with the IP address 192.168.100.33 are denied
If you want to deny certain networks then you have to specify the network IP address and the correspounding netmask for that network.

You have allowed only computers in your network to connect to your HTTP server. Now you have to allow certain users to log in and retrieve data from a dedicated directory.
This is the user-based security part.

Let's consider that **mike**, **tony** and **lynn** (all of them using computers connected to your LAN) are allowed to use your HTTP server.

- Create a file containing their names in the **/etc/httpd** directory using the following command:

   htpasswd -c /etc/httpd/http_users mike

The **-c** switch creates the **http_users** file in the aforementioned directory and also adds **mike** in this file.

- Choose a password for user **mike** when asked.

- Using the same command but without **-c** switch add the rest of the desired users to this file:

   htpasswd /etc/httpd/http_users tony
   htpasswd /etc/httpd/http_users lynn

- Create a group file **/etc/httpd/http_group_file** directory and edit it by add in this file something similar to this :

```
HTTP_Group:  mike  tony  lynn
```

You can use any name you want for the file containing names of the users allowed to access your HTTP server, as also for the group file or the name of the aforementioned group.

Open with your preferred text editor the main configuration file (**/etc/httpd/conf/httpd.conf**) of the Apache Web Server, navigate in **Section 2** of this file and find the following entry:

```
DocumentRoot "/var/www/html"
```

Modify it according to the requirements of this exercise:

```
DocumentRoot "/var/www/html/example"
```

Then find the following entry in the same section of this file:

```
<Directory "/var/www/html/">
```

It's the beginning of the container in which are specified various settings for the default directory used by Apache to serve files from.

Modify it according to the requirements of this exercise into:

```
<Directory "/var/www/html/example">
```

Beneath the last line of this file add a new container like this:

```
<Directory  "/var/www/html/example">
        AuthType Basic
        AuthName "Type your name and password bellow"
        AuthUserFile  /etc/httpd/http_users
        AuthGroupFile  /etc/httpd/http_group_file
        Require group HTTP_Group
</Directory>
```

Save settings and exit the text editor.

- Create the directory named **example** in the default location from where the Apache Web Server serves it's files.

mkdir /var/www/html/example

Create some files in the **/var/www/html/example** directory

- Start or restart your HTTP server with your new settings.

   service httpd start or **service httpd restart**

- If necessary, be sure the server will start any time you'll reboot the computer.

   chkconfig httpd on

Now it's time to test your Apache Web Server!
From another Virtual Machine or another computer, open the Internet browser and type in the IP address of your HTTP server.
For example if server's IP address is 192.168.100.100 you should type in your Internet browser **http://192.168.100.100**

Replace the IP address in my example with the IP address provided for your server. You should be able to login and browse the directory named **example** typing in the dialog box any user name with the correspounding password previously added.

Observations
*If you see only the Apache Server' welcome page but not your **example** directory, I remind you to use a text editor to open the **/etc/httpd/conf.d/ welcome.conf** file and add the pound character in front of all entries. You'll see this instruction presented at the beginning of that file also.*

*In case you want to configure this server to be a secure one (HTTPS) you have to open with a text editor the **/etc/httpd/conf.d/ssl.conf** file and make sure that the entry **Listen 443** is activated (the pound character was revomed from in front of it).*

*All directives in the **/etc/httpd/conf.d/ssl.conf** file are automatically included into Apache Web Server configuration.*
*The following directive in the **/etc/httpd/conf/httpd.conf** file reflects this action by default:*

```
#Load config files from the config directory "/etc/httpd/conf.d".
Include conf.d/*.conf
```

You can allow one single user to access your HTTP (HTTPS) server.
In this case all settings are the same as described previously except
you don't have to create the group file anymore (in my example the
/etc/httpd/http_group_file) so the aforementioned container should look like this:

```
<Directory  "/var/www/html/example">
        AuthType Basic
        AuthName "Type your name and password bellow"
        AuthUserFile  /etc/httpd/http_users
        Require user user_name
</Directory>
```

*In this example, **user_name** is the name of the user you want to be able to*
connect to your HTTP (HTTPS) server.

If you want to practice with Firewall enabled and/or SELinux enabled
*you'll have to type from a terminal **system-config-securitylevel** or, if*
*you prefer to work from GUI, go to **System**, choose **Administration**,*
*then **Security Level and Firewall** and check both boxes **Secure WWW**
*(HTTPS)** and **WWW (HTTP)** so Firewall will allow connections through*
ports 80 and 443.

*As for SELinux, if it is enabled at any level (**Enforcing** or **Permissive**) you*
need to change the ACL security context of the directory from where your
Apache Server will serve the information.
The easiest way to configure it so users will have access to your Web Server
*is to use **SELinux Troubleshooter** from GUI and comply with the indications*
you'll receive there regarding the functionality of your Apache Web Server.
In a later chapter I'll present how SELinux works.

Web access to user's home directory

The main configuration file of the Web Server gives you the possibility to let
anyone you want access a user's home directory.

For example I will assume that on you server there is a user named **mike**.
Mike created in his home directory a public directory he wants to serve
information from using the Web Server.
I will assume that this is the **/home/mike/public** directory.

For the purpose of this exercise disable Firewall and SELinux

- First you'll have to make mike's home directory executable.

  chmod 701 /home/mike

- Then you have to create the **/home/mike/public** directory and make all content in this directory readable and executable.

  chmod 705 /home/mike/public/*

- Modify using a text editor the correspounding entries in the Apache configuration file as follows:

  Establish the DocumentRoot for this example

  ```
  DocumentRoot  "/home/mike/public"
  ```

The container that settings are applied for should be now:

```
<Directory "/home/mike/public">
```

Find the entry `#UserDir enable`, activate it by removing the pound sign and edit it according to mike's directory so the entry will look like this:

```
UserDir public
```

At this point you can go forward and limit access to mike's public directory by host, allowing for example only computers in mike's network to connect to this server and/or limit access by user, specifying users that are allowed to retrieve information from mike's public directory.

When you're done with all settings, save your work and exit the text editor.

- Start you server and make sure it will be initiated in case your machine will have to be restarted.

  service httpd start and **chkconfig httpd on**

- Verify your work by accessing your Apache Server from another computer or Virtual Machine.
  Use the Internet browser in GUI or if you're in a terminal, use **links** command and type in your server's IP address.

Observations

In case you'll want Firewall enabled, I remind you to leave the traffic open through ports 80 and 443.

SELinux has to be configured to allow HTTPD to read home directories.

setsebool -P httpd_enable_homedirs 1

*The ACL settings on **/home/mike/public** must be changed too.*
*To see the ACL settings run the **ls -Z /home/mike** command.*
Change these settings by running this command:
chcon -R -u system_u -t httpd_sys_content_t /home/mike/public

*I remind you that all examples presented here refer to a basic configuration of the Apache Web Server. You can find more documentation at **http://httpd.apache.org***

Virtual hosts

A very useful feature of Apache server is that with only one IP address you can host multiple web sites on the same server.
In other words, multiple domain names could be linked to a single IP address by configuring virtual hosts.

Exercise
Configure an Apache Web Server so it will host 2 web sites:
www.number_one.test and **www.number_two.test**
Be sure Firewall and SELinux are not enabled for this exercise.

- You'll need to establish from where these web sites will serve the information.

For a better understanding I'll create for every web site a directory associating it's name with the name of the respective web site.

Because the exercise doesn't specify where to create these directories, I'll use the **/var/www/html** directory.

> **mkdir /var/www/html/number_one**
> **mkdir /var/www/html/number_two**

To verify your work later, create in each directory a html file and put some text in it.

> **touch /var/www/html/number_one/index.html** and add this text:
>
> *I AM NUMBER ONE*
>
> **touch /var/www/html/number_two/index.html** and add this text:
>
> *I AM NUMBER TWO*

* Open with a text editor the **/etc/httpd/conf/httpd.conf** file.
  Section 3 of this file refers to Virtual Hosts.
  Find the entry `#NameVirtualHost *:80` and remove the pond character:

  `NameVirtualHost *:80`

* Using the example presented at the bottom of the configuration file, you can create now a container for each of your web sites.

I'll just copy and replace accordingly the entries contained in the aforementioned example making sure they are enabled:

```
#<VirtualHost *:80>
#       ServerAdmin webmaster@dummy-host.example.com
#       DocumentRoot /www/docs/dummy-host.example.com
#       ServerName   dummy-host.example.com
#       ErrorLog logs/dummy-host.example.com-error_log
#       CustomLog logs/dummy-host.example.com-access_log common
#</VirtualHost>

<VirtualHost *:80>
        ServerAdmin root@number_one.test
        DocumentRoot /var/www/html/number_one
        ServerName   www.number_one.test
        ErrorLog logs/www.number_one.test-error_log
        CustomLog logs/www.number_one.test-access_log common
</VirtualHost>
```

```
<VirtualHost *:80>
        ServerAdmin root@number_two.test
        DocumentRoot /var/www/html/number_two
        ServerName    www.number_two.test
        ErrorLog logs/www.number_two.test-error_log
        CustomLog logs/www.number_two.test-access_log common
</VirtualHost>
```

Observation

In this exercise the directive referring to ServerAdmin *may be suspended because you don't have a configured mail service and a fully qualified domain name.*

- Check if modifications you made in the main configuration file are correct. From a terminal type the following command:

    httpd -S

If no mistakes were done while editing, you should see a response like this:

```
[root@localhost ~]# httpd -S
VirtualHost configuration:
wildcard NameVirtualHosts and _default_ servers:
_default_:443 localhost.localdomain
/etc/httpd/conf.d/ssl.conf:81)
*:80                is a NameVirtualHost
default server www.number_one.test
(/etc/httpd/conf/httpd.conf:993)
port 80 namevhost www.number_one.test
(/etc/httpd/conf/httpd.conf:993)
port 80 namevhost www.number_two.test
(/etc/httpd/conf/httpd.conf:1001)
```

- Start or restart the httpd daemon:

    service httpd start or **service httpd restart**

    Eventually be sure it will start automatically in case you'll need to reboot your computer.

    chkconfig httpd on

Time to access your virtual web sites!

Assuming that you'll access these virtual web sites from a Linux® machine, you need to edit the **/etc/hosts** file of the remote machine by adding two entries as in the following example:

```
# Do not remove the following line, or various programs
# that require network functionality will fail.
127.0.0.1         localhost.localdomain localhost
::1               localhost6.localdomain6 localhost6
192.168.49.130    www.number_one.test
192.168.49.130    www.number_two.test
```

As you've noticed, this entries will instruct the remote machine to look for your virtual sites at the same IP address.
You have to do this as long as you don't have a fully qualified domain name (FQDN).
In other words you'll have to instruct DNS to look for these virtual websites by binding the IP address to the names of the web sites.
In a following chapter I'll also present some basics of the DNS and how to configure a DNS server.

Don't forget to replace the IP address used in my example with the IP address of your HTTP server !

Use the Internet browser or **links** command and type in
www.number_one.test and then **http://www.number_two.test**
You should be able to see successively the text added in each of the **index.html** files created before.

Configuring secure Virtual Hosts

For a better understanding, I'll use the previously presented example to configure this time two secure web sites.
Again, I'll remind you to disable Firewall and SELinux for this exercise.

Exercise
Configure your Apache Server to host two secure web sites named
www.number_one.test and **www.number_two.test**

Before beginning this exercise I suggest to use as DocumentRoot a different directory, other than the default **/var/www/html** directory of the web server.

> **make /secure_web**
> **make /secure_web/number_one**
> **touch /secure_web/number_one/index.html** and put some text in it.
>
> **make /secure_web/number_two**
> **touch /secure_web/number_two/index.html** and put some text in this file.

* Open with a text editor the **/etc/httpd/conf/httpd.conf** file and modify
  it as follows:

Suspend the directive Listen 80

Listen 80

Edit the DocumentRoot section to reflect the requirements of this exercise:

DocumentRoot "/secure_web"

Modify the name of the container so the host-based security directives will refer properly to your DocumentRoot:

<DocumentRoot "/secure_web">

Suspend the directive NameVirtualHost *:80

NameVirtualHost *:80

Observation
*Because the secure web server uses **TCP port 443** to accept connections you don't want any traffic through the default **TCP port 80** so you need to suspend both* Listen 80 *and* NameVirtualHost *:80 *directives.*

* Open with a text editor the **/etc/httpd/conf.d/ssl.conf** file and modify
  it as follows:

Find the Listen 443 directive and make sure it is active:

```
Listen 443
```

Add beneath it the following directive:

```
NameVirtualHost *:443
```
                        or
```
NameVirtualHost _default_:443
```

This way you'll instruct Apache to use only the secure **TCP port 443** for incoming traffic.

Notice in this file the container referring to `<VirtualHost _default_:443>` and the security directives included.
You have to duplicate this container in **/etc/httpd/conf.d/ssl.conf** file so in the end you'll obtain two similar containers that will be modified to reflect settings for your both secure web sites specified in this exercise as in the following example:

```
<VirtualHost _default_:443>
# General setup for the virtual host, inherited from global
configuration
DocumentRoot "/secure_web/number_one/"
ServerName www.number_one.test:443
# Use separate log files for the SSL virtual host; note that
LogLevel
# is not inherited from httpd.conf.
ErrorLog logs/ssl_error_log
TransferLog logs/ssl_access_log
LogLevel warn
SSLEngine on
SSLProtocol all -SSLv2
SSLCipherSuite ALL:!ADH:!EXPORT:!SSLv2:RC4+RSA:+HIGH:+MEDIUM:+LOW
SSLCertificateFile /etc/pki/tls/certs/localhost.crt
SSLCertificateKeyFile /etc/pki/tls/private/localhost.key
<Files ~ "\.(cgi|shtml|phtml|php3?)$">
    SSLOptions +StdEnvVars
</Files>
<Directory "/var/www/cgi-bin">
    SSLOptions +StdEnvVars
</Directory>
SetEnvIf User-Agent ".*MSIE.*" \
        nokeepalive ssl-unclean-shutdown \
        downgrade-1.0 force-response-1.0
CustomLog logs/ssl_request_log \
        "%t %h %{SSL_PROTOCOL}x %{SSL_CIPHER}x \"%r\" %b"
</VirtualHost>
```

```
<VirtualHost _default_:443>
# General setup for the virtual host, inherited from global
configuration
DocumentRoot "/secure_web/number_two/"
ServerName www.number_two.test:443
ErrorLog logs/ssl_error_log
TransferLog logs/ssl_access_log
LogLevel warn
SSLEngine on
SSLProtocol all -SSLv2
SSLCipherSuite ALL:!ADH:!EXPORT:!SSLv2:RC4+RSA:+HIGH:+MEDIUM:+LOW

SSLCertificateFile /etc/pki/tls/certs/localhost.crt
SSLCertificateKeyFile /etc/pki/tls/private/localhost.key
<Files ~ "\.(cgi|shtml|phtml|php3?)$">
    SSLOptions +StdEnvVars
</Files>
<Directory "/var/www/cgi-bin">
    SSLOptions +StdEnvVars
</Directory>
SetEnvIf User-Agent ".*MSIE.*" \
         nokeepalive ssl-unclean-shutdown \
         downgrade-1.0 force-response-1.0
CustomLog logs/ssl_request_log \
         "%t %h %{SSL_PROTOCOL}x %{SSL_CIPHER}x \"%r\" %b"

</VirtualHost>
```

Observation

As you can see, I have removed the comments but same directives were kept for both containers replacing accordingly DocumentRoot *and* ServerName *for each secure web site.*

Before continuing let's analyze this two entries in Apache secure configuration file:

```
SSLCertificateFile /etc/pki/tls/certs/localhost.crt
SSLCertificateKeyFile /etc/pki/tls/private/localhost.key
```

They indicate paths to specific files that hold the **SSL Certificates.**
The SSL (Secure Socket Layer) Certificates consist in a pair of encrypted files one used for encrypting and the other one used to decrypt the information exchanged between your Apache Server and a client (a web browser).

You can conclude that the two entries mentioned in the **/etc/httpd/conf.d/ssl.conf** file will determined the Apache daemon to look for the pair cypher-key in order to start this application under secure circumstances.

Check the files **/etc/pki/tls/certs/localhost.crt** and **/etc/pki/tls/private/localhost.key** to see what contains.

If both of these files exist, the command **httpd -S** should return no error in the answer. If you don't have these files you can generate them using the **genkey** command.

genkey localhost

You should see a message like this:

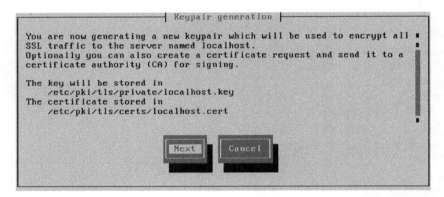

Then by pressing **Next** on this screen another dialog box will appear asking you to choose the sise of your key.

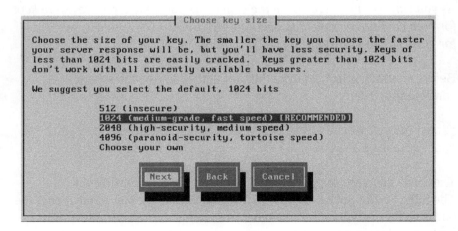

After you have selected the size, next dialog box will show you a progress bar indicating the status of generating the keys.

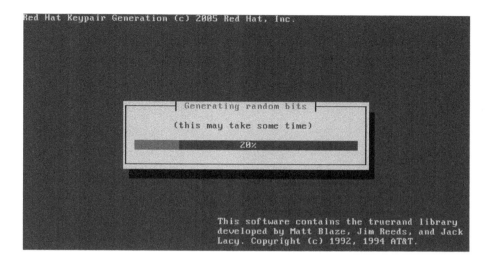

When this is done and if you have a fully qualified domain name, the next dialog box will ask you if you want to send a Certificate Request to a Certificate Authority. For this exercise select **No.**

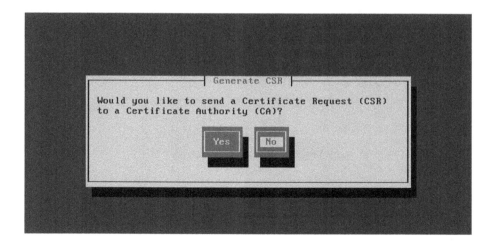

Next dialog box will require some information for your certificate.
I suggest not to modify these fields for the purpose if this exercise.

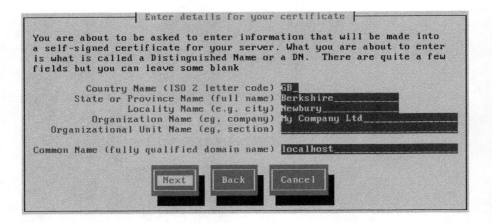

Next you'll need to decide if you want to protect your key or not by selecting
or leaving deselected the field **Encrypt the private key.**

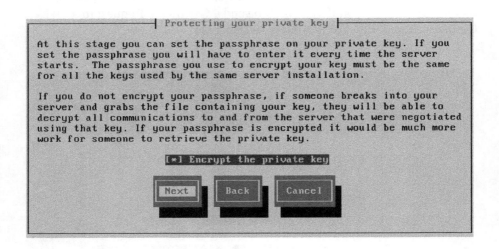

Introduce a password as requested:

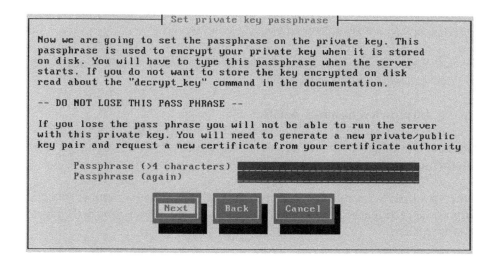

Remember that every time you have to restart Apache server, you'll be prompted to introduce this password. So don't forget it!

After the SSL Certificates were generated issue the **ls -l** command to list them in the specified directories.
 Now, pay attention to the file named **localhost.cert** generated with the aforementioned command.
If you'll want to start Apache now, probably you'll receive an error message stating that the file **/etc/pki/tsl/certs/localhost.crt** doesn't exist or it's empty!

This happens because the **genkey** command created a file named **localhost.cert** and the **/etc/httpd/conf.d/ssl.conf** file instructs Apache Server through it's directive **SSLCertificateFile /etc/pki/tls/certs/localhost.crt** to look for a different file, named as you can see **localhost.crt.**

So modify this entry making sure it will be:

SSLCertificateFile /etc/pki/tls/certs/localhost.cert

- Start your server eventually make sure it will start also next time your server will be restarted:

  service httpd start or/and **chkconfig httpd on**

For testing your work go to a different computer or a different Virtual Machine and edit the **/etc/hosts** file adding, as in the previous example, two entries specifying the unique IP address that binds the names of your secure virtual hosts to the IP address of your Apache Server.

Open the Internet browser of the remote machine and try first to type in one of your web sites addresses like this:

http://www.number_one.test

Notice the response and remember what directives you have suspended in the **/etc/httpd/conf/http.conf** file

Now type **https://www.number_one.test**, eventually **https://www.number_two.test.** Import the certificates as instructed and then you should see your web pages created earlier.

The Red Hat httpd configuration tool

Red Hat® Enterprise Linux® based distributions present also a graphical tool to help you configure the Apache Server.
Activate this tool by issuing from a terminal **system-config-httpd** command or go to **System**, choose **Administration**, **Server Settings** and click on **HTTP**.

When using this graphical tool, any configuration existing in the **/etc/httpd/conf/httpd.conf** file will be overwritten.

This tool has however some limitations. In case you'll want to configure a secure Web Server you still have to manually edit the **/etc/httpd/conf.d/ssl.conf** file.

As for the virtual hosts part, it provides explicit steps for configuring secure or non secure web sites. Just hit the Virtual Hosts tab and you'll have all options to configure your desired type of virtual hosts.

You can try now this tool using the same data as in the previous exercise and then analyze both files **/etc/httpd/conf/httpd.conf** and **/etc/httpd/conf.d/ssl. conf** to see how options were set.

I remind you to consult Apache's log files in **/var/log/httpd** directory if you suspect problems especially security violations so you could intervene as fast as possible to block any unwanted access to your server.

The Squid Caching Proxy Server

Squid server, also known as Web proxy cache server has the ability to improve network connection.
Using the Inter-Cache Protocol (ICP) stores information from visited web sites or files offering users the possibility to retrieve the necessary information without searching it on Internet.
This is an important advantage in case of large and busy networks where clients are looking all the time for big amount of data over Internet.

Once the desired data is accessed, Squid will store it in it's cache so next time when someone in that network will want to retrieve the same information again, Squid will point the client computer to it's cache saving this way a lot of bandwidth so other computers will be able to connect faster to Internet.

The main configuration file for Squid is **/etc/squid/squid.conf** and the log files are located in **/var/squid directory.**

If you have installed the package Web Server with a command like **yum groupinstall "Web Server"** then both services Apache and Squid are already installed.

Check it's existence with the **rpm -qa | grep squid** command.

If it's not installed already then you can use **yum install squid** command or the Package Manager tool to install Squid.

Squid Proxy Server

Squid configuration file is huge, but fortunately you have to modify only three entries in the **/etc/squid/squid.conf** file in order to configure Squid as a proxy server for your network.

- Open **/etc/squid/squid.conf** file with a text editor, search for the directive `http_port 3128` and make sure it is active.

- Search for the section referring to **visible_hostname**.
  If the name of the local computer is **localhost** then add in this section an entry that says:

  ```
  visible_hostname localhost
  ```

- Search for the title `INSERT YOUR OWN RULE(S) HERE TO ALLOW ACCESS FROM YOUR CLIENTS.`
  Here you'll see the following suspended entries:

  ```
  #acl our_networks src 192.168.1.0/24   192.168.2.0/24
  #http_access allow our_networks
  ```

These directives must be active to support regular HTTP access.

  In case you want Squid to be a proxy server for multiple networks edit these directives like this:

  ```
  acl our_networks src 192.168.49.0/24   192.168.1.0/24
  http_access allow our_networks
  ```

  If you want Squid to be a proxy server only for your network then the directives should look like this:

  ```
  acl local_net src 192.168.49.0/24
  http_access allow local_net
  ```

The IP addresses used here are just examples of network IP addresses I wanted Squid to be a proxy server for. You have to replace them properly.

- Create Squid swap directories by typing from a terminal:
  squid -z

- Start Squid and eventually make sure it starts automatically next time when you'l reboot the computer.

  service squid start and/or **chkconfig squid on**

Time to check your work!
For this, use another computer or a Virtual Machine, and open the Internet browser. If the Internet browser is Mozilla Firefox open Firefox Preferences from the menu and select **Advanced.**

Select **Network** tab and then press **Settings.**

Type in the **HTTP Proxy** box the IP address of your Squid proxy server and also don't forget to specify it's default port **3128.**
Press **OK** and then open a few web sites.

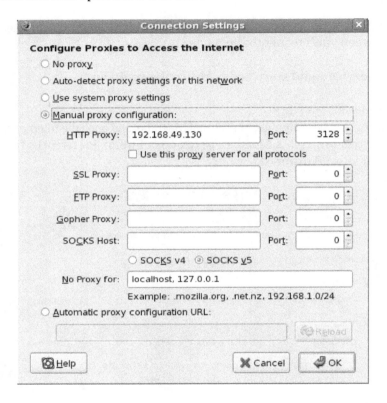

When you open for the second time the same web site you'll notice that loading the default page of that web site is done faster.

Chapter 7.　Sharing Files On Network: NFS, FTP, Samba

The Network File System (NFS) Service

The NFS service is based on exporting a filesystem generally, or to a particular network, domain or computer by editing the **/etc/exports** file in a certain way.
It relays on RPC (Remote Procedure Calls) to function.
When RPC processes start, they notify the **portmap** daemon about the program number and port they expect to serve.

A client computer will contact server's **portmap** with a particular RPC program number and then **portmap** decides toward what port number the client must be redirected.
The **portmap** daemon also reads the indications from **/etc/hosts.allow** and **/etc/hosts.deny** files handling the client's request according to these files.

In conclusion, **nfs** daemon won't start if **portmap** daemon is not already running.
Verify if **portmap** daemon is running by typing **service portmap status** from a terminal.
If the command returns a negative response then start the daemon with:

service portmap start eventually **chkconfig portmap on.**

To see the status of current RPC services, type **rpcinfo -p localhost**

Before configuring a NFS serve, first check the existence of the **nfs** and **portmap** packages on your computer. They should be included by default.

> **rpm -qa | grep nfs**
> **rpm -qa | grep portmap**

NFS server configuration

For this exercise don't enable Firewall or SELinux. Use s**ystem-config-securitylevel** to disable these services if they are active.

Exercise

Configure a NFS server to share files only in your network, from a directory named **public**, located in user's mike home directory.

- Check if packages **nfs** and **portmap** exist on your server:

  rmp -qa | grep nfs
  rpm -qa | grep portmap

- Create in mike's home directory the requested **public** directory. Eventually add some files in it.

  mkdir /home/mike/public

- Open with a text editor the **/etc/exports** file. By default this file should be empty.
  If your network's IP address is **192.168.1.0/24** add an entry like this:

  ```
  /home/mike/public    192.168.1.0/24(ro,sync)
  ```

- Save settings and exit

- Export the **/home/mike/public** directory by typing from a terminal:

  exportfs -a

- Verify the status of both daemons **nfs** and **portmap**, eventually make sure they will start automatically in case of a server reboot.

  service nfs status, service portmap status
  service nfs start, service portmap start
  chkconfig nfs on, **chkconfig portmap on**

- Verify your export list by typing from a terminal:

  showmount -e

Observations

The /etc/exports file permits the export of not only one directory or file, but as many as you like, if each directory or file about to be exported represents an entry written on one line in this file with the appropriate export options attached. In conclusion, the /etc/export file contains two columns: first column represents the path to the exported directory in your NFS server and the second column will reflect the export options of the specified directory or file.

NFS allows a various number of export options to a network or to a specific computer using the name of the host, the IP address of the host or network and wildcards.

In this exercise the entry in the /etc/exports file says that the /home/mike/public directory is exported to all computers in my network within the IP address range from 192.168.1.1 to 192.168.1.254 and the subnet mask 255.255.255.0 with the following options: ro – read only and sync – write data to disk on request.

An example of /etc/exports file:

```
/public      *.test.org(ro,insecure,sync,no_root_squash)
/home        *(ro,root_squash)
/example     192.168.0.0/24(ro,all_squash) *home.test(ro,no_wdelay)
```

The option root_squash indicates that remote root users won't have root privileges on the shared directory. These privileges will be obtained if you use the option no_root_squash for the exported directory.
If exported directory has the option all_squash, all remote users will be treated as anonymous user.

All export options are described in the man pages of exports file (man exports).

NFS Client Configuration

To test your NFS server you'll need to configure another computer or Virtual Machine to look for the shared information of the server.

You can do this by editing the /etc/fstab file of the remote machine so any time the remote machine will be restarted, it will look for the specified shared directory.

Be sure Firewall and SELinux are disabled also on the remote machine for this exercise.

- On the remote machine, open the **/etc/fstab** file and add the following entry that complies to this exercise:

```
192.168.1.100:/home/mike/public  /opt  nfs  defaults 0 0
```

Assuming that **/home/mike/public** is on the server that has the IP address 192.168.1.100 I told the remote machine to mount this directory all the time as **nfs** in it's **/opt** directory.
You can mount it in any directory you like. Don't forget to replace the IP address in my example with the IP address of the machine you had configured as your NFS server.

- Mount the shared directory on the remote machine by typing from a terminal:

   mount -a

- List on the remote machine the **/opt** directory. You should see here all files shared by the NFS server.

   ls -l /opt

Observations
On the remote machine, if you want the shared directory to be mounted all the time, it is recommended to replace the option defaults *in /etc/fstab with* soft,timeo=N *so the entry in the exercise would be:*

```
192.168.1.100:/home/mike/public   /opt   nfs   soft,timeo=N 0 0
```

*where **N** is the timeout interval expressed in tenths of seconds (*timeo=100 *means a timeout interval of **10 seconds**).*

This options are recommended to be used in /etc/fstab of the remote machine because NFS is a stateless protocol which allows the client computer to wait in case the NFS server fails.
*Because this wait could last forever it's a good idea to introduce the **timeo** and **soft** options which will cause the remote machine to fail connecting to server after the established timeout period rather then waiting.*

In case you don't want to have all the time the shared files mounted on your remote machine you could use the **automounter** service and access them only when you need.

The **automounter** service relies on the **autofs** daemon.

Assuming that you want to practice with the **automounter** on the remote machine you have already edited it's **/etc/fstab** file, you have to unmount the **/opt** directory first.

> **umount -l /opt**

If you list the content of the **/opt** directory now, it should indicate that it has no shared directory in it.

Open the **/etc/fstab** file with your preferred text editor and **delete** the entry you have added in the previous exercise:

```
192.168.1.100:/home/mike/public  /opt  nfs  defaults  0  0
```

Save settings and exit text editor.

Check if the **autofs** service is active on your remote machine:

> **service autofs status**

The **autofs** daemon should be active by default, but in case it is not active, just type:

> **service autofs start**
> and/or
> **chkconfig autofs on**

On the remote machine, open the **/etc/auto.misc** file and edit it by adding a line like this:

```
*    -ro,sync,intr        192.168.1.100:/home/mike/public
```

As you can see, the **/etc/auto.misc** file offers you some examples regarding how you can mount on your machine different NFS directories of files.

The entry I've added in this file says that the directory **/home/mike/public** shared by the machine who's IP is **192.168.1.100**, will be mounted on the remote machine with certain properties (**ro,sync,intr**).

But where will be mounted that directory?

Take a look into the **/etc/auto.master** on the remote machine.

By default it should be a sample **auto.master** file in your machine which will be used by the **autofs** service to mount any shared directory via NFS into a directory you'll decide on the remote machine.

If you'll want to mount the shared directory into **/misc** on the remote machine you'll have to edit the /etc/auto.master by adding this entry:

```
/misc           /etc/auto.misc
```

Restart the **autofs** service on the remote machine by typing from a terminal **service autofs restart** and change directory into **/misc/192.168.1.100.**

If you list now this directory, you'll see in it the directory shared by your NFS server.

ls -l /misc/192.168.1.100

NFS Server Configuration Tool

Red Hat Enterprise Linux based distributions provide also this graphical tool to help you configure a NFS server.
You can initiate this tool by typing from a terminal **system-config-nfs** or go in **System**, choose **Administration, Server Settings** and then **NFS.**

If you press the **Add** button, a dialog window will open giving you the possibility to establish what directories you want to share and what options you want to use for them by selecting between the appropriate tabs in this window.
General Options and **User Access** tabs will provide the mounting options.

It might be a good idea to practice configuring a NFS server using the graphical tool selecting from these tabs different mounting options and then analyze the **/etc/exports** file while consulting in parallel the aforementioned man pages for this file.
This way you'll have a better understanding over the mounting options and in time you'll know exactly what options you will have to choose given a real situation.

Let's have a closer look at the **Server Settings** menu:

As I have mentioned at the beginning of this chapter, the **nfs daemon** relays on RPC services to start.
If you want to configure your NFS server to work through Firewall you have to make sure that all necessary services related to NFS will accept connections from remote machines through their specific ports, or different ports you might want to specify.

Assuming that your NFS server is up and running, from a terminal type :

rpcinfo –p localhost

The output should reveal something like this :

```
[root@localhost ~]# rpcinfo -p localhost
      program          vers        proto  port
      100000            2           tcp   111      portmapper
      100000            2           udp   111      portmapper
      100024            1           udp   604      status
      100024            1           tcp   607      status
      100003            2           udp   2049     nfs
      100003            3           udp   2049     nfs
      100003            4           udp   2049     nfs
      100021            1           udp   59762    nlockmgr
      100021            3           udp   59762    nlockmgr
      100021            4           udp   59762    nlockmgr
      100003            2           tcp   2049     nfs
      100003            3           tcp   2049     nfs
      100003            4           tcp   2049     nfs
      100021            1           tcp   44172    nlockmgr
      100021            3           tcp   44172    nlockmgr
      100021            4           tcp   44172    nlockmgr
      100005            1           udp   694      mountd
      100005            1           tcp   697      mountd
      100005            2           udp   694      mountd
      100005            2           tcp   697      mountd
      100005            3           udp   694      mountd
      100005            3           tcp   697      mountd
      100011            1           udp   910      rquotad
      100011            2           udp   910      rquotad
      100011            1           tcp   913      rquotad
      100011            2           tcp   913      rquotad
```

This display helps you determine what daemons must be active as also the ports they are using in order to have a functional NFS server through Firewall.

Notice that all daemons displayed here use **TCP** (Transmission Control Protocol) and **UDP** (User Datagram Protocol) protocols, so be sure to instruct Firewall to accept connections though both of these ports for all services **nfs daemon** is relaying on!

The **Server Settings** menu offers you the possibility to designate different port numbers for the specified daemons.

There are a series of directives that SELinux uses regarding the NFS server. These directives have to be set according to the export options you have set for the desired exported files or directories in your NFS server.
The **/selinux/boolians** directory contains, among others, all directives referring toNFS.
For example, if you want SELinux to support read-write to NFS shared directories, you can use the following command:

setsebool -P nfs_export_all_rw 1

The File Transfer Protocol (FTP) Service

Another method of sharing files over network is by using the FTP service. For downloading/uploading files with this service, a client computer contacts the FTP server which (depending of server's configuration) will prompt the client for user name and password.

Very Secure FTP server configuration (vsFTP)

First you have to install the necessary packages.
Assuming that you have an active Internet connection you can use **Pirut** or **yum** to obtain the **vsftpd** package:

yum install vsftpd

Once installed, you'll find the main configuration file in **/etc/vsftpd/vsftpd.conf.** Save this configuration file before modifying it !

By default, the **vsFTP** service uses **/var/ftp/pub** directory to serve files.

If you'll add some files in **/var/ftp/pub** directory and start the server with the **service vsftpd start** command, (don't forget to disable **Firewall** and **SELinux** before starting the server!) anyone knowing your FTP server's IP address is able to access the files you have just created in the default directory.

A closer look inside the **/etc/vsftpd/vsftpd.conf** file will reveal a list of entries that control the behavior of the FTP server, each entry having a pretty clear description.

However, I'll insist on a few entries that may cause problems if not understood correctly.

```
#chroot_list_enable=YES

# (default follows)
#chroot_list_file=/etc/vsftpd/chroot_list
```

As you notice, these entries are not activated by default (they start with a pound character in front).

If you want to activate the **chroot_list_enable** directive, you must create in **/etc/vsftpd** directory a file named **chroot_list** as suggested by the directive **chroot_list_file** which must also be activated.
You can add in the **chroot_list** file names of desired users previously added on your computer.

For example, assuming that you have already added on your computer the following users: **mike**, **nick**, **john** and for each one of these users you also created a login password, now you can add the same users in the **chroot_list** file by typing one name per line.

Then you can edit the **/etc/vsftpd/vsftpd.conf** file by modifying, for example, only the following directives leaving the default directives unmodified:

```
anonymus_enable=NO

chroot_list_enable=YES

chroot_list_file=/etc/vsftpd/chroot_list
```

Once **anonymus_enable** is set to **NO**, any client trying to access your FTP server will be prompted for user name and password.

Activating **chroot_list_enable** directive and also setting it to **YES,** this requires to be activated also the **chroot_list_file** directive which instructs the FTP server where to find the **chroot_list** file (in our case the path to the aforementioned file is **/etc/vsftpd/chroot_list**).

What exactly **chroot_list_enable** directive does?

When this directive is active (the pound character is removed from in front of the entry) and set to **YES**, the FTP server will read the users you added in **chroot_list** file (the example was **mike, nick, john**) and after they will be prompted to introduce the user name and password, once login successful, these users specified in the mentioned list will be "sent to jail" in their own **/home** directory.

This means that after login **mike** will be able to access, read and modify only files located in **/home/mike, nick** will be able to access, read and modify only files located in **/home/nick**, etc.

The directive **userlist_enable**, active and set to **YES** by default works together with the directive **userlist_deny** – that you have to add in the default configuration file **/etc/vsftpd/vsftpd.conf**

How **userlist_enable** and **userlist_deny** work?

    a)   If   `userlist_enable=YES`
           and
          `userlist_deny=YES`

the FTP server reads the list of users **/etc/vsftpd/user_list** and *will not allow these users* to login. This is the default setting.

    b)   If   `userlist_enable=YES`
           and
          `userlist_deny=NO`

the FTP server reads the list of users **/etc/vsftpd/user_list** and *will allow only these users* to login.

The **tcp_wrappers** directive set to **YES** by default indicates that your FTP server follows the rules established in **/etc/hosts.allow** or **/etc/hosts.deny** files.

The **local_root** directive helps you change the default directory **/var/ftp/pub** into any other directory you choose.
In other words, if you don't want to "serve" your files from the default **/var/ftp/pub** directory, add this directive into the default **/etc/vsftpd/vsftpd. conf** file, specifying the path to a desired directory.

      local_root=/path/to/my/desired/directory

Example: **local_root=/home/test**, or **local_root=/test**

Observation
Changing the default FTP's directory with `local_root` *directive is possible if* `anonymus_enable` *directive is set to* NO*.*

Exercise
Create a vsFTP server where users can only access files located in their home directories from any computer in your network.
To complete this exercise I'll consider the users mentioned before: **mike**, **nick** and **john.**

- Assuming that you have already installed the necessary rpm package for this exercise, and also Firewall and SELinux are disabled, open the **/etc/vsftpd/vsftpd.conf** file and edit, eventually activate only the following enties:

```
anonymus_enable=NO
chroot_list_enable=YES
chroot_list_file=/etc/vsftpd/chroot_list
```

- Use your favorite text editor to create in **/etc/vsftpd** directory the file named **chroot_list** and add the desired user names in it. In this case: **mike**, **nick** and **john** (one user per line) :

```
mike
nick
john
```

When you're done save settings end exit the text editor

- Start your server, eventually make it start every time you'll reboot your computer.

  service vsftpd start and/or **chkconfig vsftpd on**

- Access your server from another computer by typing in your Internet Browser the IP address of the FTP server.
  My server's IP address is **192.168.1.100** so the command will be:

  ftp://192.168.1.100

Replace this IP address according to your server's IP.

The Samba Services

The Samba service allows you to share directories and/or printers with
Windows® or other Linux® computers.
If you have selected **Windows File Server** when you've installed your
Linux® distribution, then Samba rpm packages were installed too.

If you missed that use **Pirut** to select the mentioned package group or **yum**

    yum install samba

The configuration file for Samba is **/etc/samba/smb.conf** file.
Don't forget to save a copy of this file before editing it!

a) Configuring Samba server to share directories and printers with Linux® client computers

I'll explain how you have to do such configuration using an exercise.

Exercise
Allow users **user_1** and **user_2** located on different remote computers in
you network, to access the **/test** directory and the printer shared by your
Samba server.

* You'll need to add these users to your Samba server and also to
  assign a Samba password for each one of them when prompted:

    useradd -Mn user_1
    smbpasswd -a user_1

    useradd -Mn user_2
    smbpasswd -a user_2

Observation
*Given the fact that **user_1** and **user_2** are "external" users of my Samba
server, I've added them to my computer without creating a home directory
(operator -M) or a group (operator -n) for any of them.*

- Open with a text editor the **/etc/samba/sbm.conf** file edit and activate (by removing the semi colon at the beginning of the respective line) the following entries as follows:

`workgroup = MYGROUP`	- this is default. You can replace MYGROUP with any name you like as long as the remote computers have the same value as the server established for this entry in their **/etc/samba/smb.conf** file.
`netbios name =`	- insert here the IP address of your Samba server. Don't forget to activate it by removing the semi colon (;)
`hosts allow =`	- insert here the IP of your network as the exercise requires.

Example:
If your network IP is **192.168.1.0** then `hosts allow = 192.168.1.0/24` or `hosts allow = 192.168.1.`
Also see the examples offered in the configuration file regarding this entry.

Observation
If you want your Samba server to share files with computers from other known domains or networks you can also add on the same line the IP address of the desired computer or network.
Of course, you will also have to add the respective user names as I have showed you at the beginning of this exercise.

- Find the section `[printers]` which by default should contain the following active entries:

```
comment = All Printers
path = /var/spool/samba
browseable = no
guest ok = no
writable = no
printable = yes
```

If your Samba configuration file contains the same entries for this section, then any printer connected to your server is properly shared.

- At the bottom of the configuration file you'll find an example – **[public]** - of how to share a directory.

Based on this example I have added in **/etc/samba/smb.conf** file the following requirements for my exercise:

```
[test]
comment = my samba shared directory
path = /test
browseable = yes
public = yes
writable = yes
guest ok = no
valid users = user_1 user_2
```

Observation
Because Linux® distributions were developed along time by people around the world that don't use currently the English language don't correct the entry written "browseable". Samba will read it as it is and will share properly the desired directory.

- Save your settings and exit the text editor

Time to check your work !

Open a terminal on you server and type: **testparm**
The command will load the settings of your Samba server and also will provide a dump of your server definitions.
If everything looks good, start your Samba server by typing from a terminal:

service smb start eventually **chkconfig smb on**

Go to a remote machine, open a terminal and issue a command like this :

smbclient //you_server_IP_address/test -U user_name

If your server's IP address is **192.168.1.100** and you want to login as **user_1** then you'll have to type :

> **smbclient //192.168.1.100/test -U user_1**

You'll be prompted to introduce **user_1**'s password. If you see a prompter like this `smb:\>` then you're logged in !
Now you can place, retrieve, remove, list files in the **/test** directory. For a complete set of available commands just type **help** from the prompter.

Placing a file named **test_file** located in the home directory of an user on the server is done issuing a command like this :

> `smb:\>` **put /home/user_name/test_file test_file**

Retrieving a file from the server is done issuing a command like this:

> `smb:\>` **get test_file**

b) Configuring Samba server to share directories and printers with Windows® client computers.

Linux® is known for it's flexibility, so probably you have figured out by now that if your network includes Linux® and also Windows® computers, setting up your Samba server to share directories and printers with such mixture of operating systems has to be done pretty much in the same manner as in the previous exercise.

All you have to do is to follow exactly the same steps I have described in the previous exercise and eventually when you'll edit the **/etc/samba/smb.conf** file, activate the entry `wins support = yes` in the **Name Resolution** section. I remind you that to activate this entry you'll have to remove the semi colon (**;**) from in front of it.

Make sure the same value for **workgroup** is established for Windows® computers as also for Linux® computers.
Usually Windows® computers will have established by default the value **WORKGROUP** for **workgroup**.

The Samba Server Configuration Tool

This graphical tool provided by the Red Hat® Enterprise Linux® based distributions helps you configure the Samba server.

You can start this tool either from a terminal by typing **system-config-samba** either go to **Settings**, choose **Administration**, **Server Settings** and then click on **Samba.**

In the menu that opens select **Preferences** then **Samba Users.**
Press **Add User** button to add the users according to the requirements of the exercise described in this section.

Note that **user_ 1** is able to connect to my Samba server from a Red Hat® Enterprise Linux® machine and also from a Windows® machine using a unique password.

You'll have to add **user_2** following the same steps.

When you're done adding users go to **Preferences** and choose **Server Settings.**

You'll notice that the new menu had two tabs : **Basic** and **Security**.
In the **Basic** Tab you'll be able to establish the value for **Workgroup** and also a description of your Samba server.

Activating the **Security** tab you can set different security parameters.

Notice that **Authentication Mode** is set to **User** and **Guest Account** is set for **No guest account.**

Up to now I have added users to my Samba server, I have established passwords for users so they ca log into my server from a Linux® machine and also from a Windows® machine.
More than that, I have set different parameters for Samba server.
It's time to add the desired shared directory **/test** to my server.

For this, click on **Add Share** button and notice in the menu that opens two tabs: **Basic** and **Access**.

The Basic tab gives you the possibility to add the **/test** directory and to set some basic parameters for it:

In the **Access** tab you can choose the users you want to have access to the
/test directory.
I have highlighted the **Only allow access to specific users** option and I have
selected **user_1** from the list.

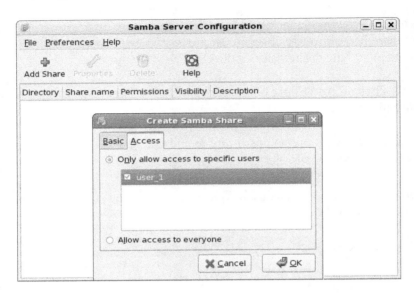

Click **OK** and take a look at the shared **/test** directory by your Samba server.

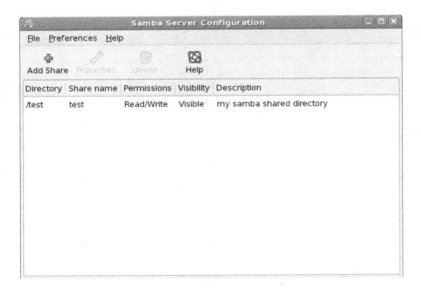

Your Samba server is up and running sharing the **/test** directory.

But what about the printer?

All you have to do is go back to **System**, choose **Administration** then click on **Printing**.
In the menu that opens choose **Server Setting**s and check the box **Share published printers connected to this system**.

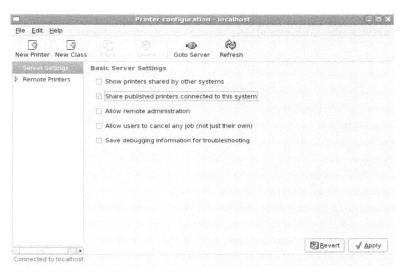

Click **Apply** and now the requirements of the previous exercise are totally met!

I find proper to explain now how a Linux® client computer can gain access to shared folders by a Samba server using a graphic tool.

As a Linux® client, in this situation all you have to do is hit **Alt** and **F2** keys together and type in a command under this form:

smb://username:password@samba_server/shared_directory

Replace **username** and **password** in this expression with the user name and password of your users, replace **samba_server** with the IP address of your Samba Server and **shared_directory** with the name of the shared directory (according to our exercise this will be **/test**).

If you want to access a shared directory located on a Windows® machine, on your Linux® computer press **Alt** and **F2** and type in a command like this :

smb://192.168.1.200/shared_directory

I have considered **192.168.1.200** as being the IP address of the Windows®
machine you want to access.

Another method to access a Windows® computer that shares certain
directories on the network is by going to **Places** on your Linux® machine and
choose **Connect to server.**

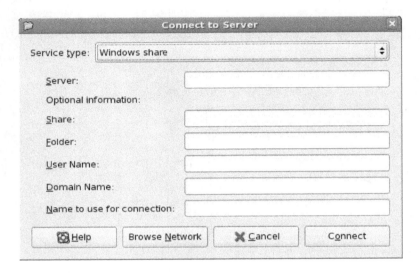

For the **Service type** choose **Windows share**, insert the IP address of the
Windows® computer you want to access and eventually fill in the **Optional
information section.**
When you're done click **Connect.**

Chapter 8:   Mail Server

A Mail Server needs three important components in order to function: a Mail Transfer Agent (**MTA**), a Mail Delivery Agent (**MDA**) and a Mail User Agent (**MUA**).
The only component that you'll have to install is the desired MTA, while the other two are already installed.

The Mail Transfer Agent is a software that relays on the **SMTP** (Simple Mail Transfer Protocol) daemon to transfer electronic mail messages from one computer to another.
In this chapter I will describe how to configure a Mail Server using **dovecot** and **sendmail.**

A Mail Delivery Agent is the software that delivers the electronic mail messages into the mailboxes of the recipients. The most popular MDA on Linux® systems are **procmail** and **maildrop**.

The Mail User Agent is the computer program used to manage the e-mails. A client of a mail server could use mail, Evolution or Thunderbird to manage it's electronic mail messages.

Mail Server Configuration – Dovecot and Sendmail

First I'll remind you that to deliver mail, **Dovecot** uses **POP3** (Post Office Protocol version 3), **IMAP** (Internet Message Access Protocol) as also the secure versions of these protocols - **POP3S** and **IMAPS.**

Electronic mail messages coming from an **MTA** are stored on the mail server. If the server is configured to use **POP**, then a client application (mail, Evolution, Thunderbird) will download the mail messages from the **POP** server to be further processed on the respective local host.

If the mail server is configured to use **IMAP** then all electronic mail messages will be maintained on the **IMAP** server as a database. This protocol is mostly used for the Web based mail services.

Before installing and configuring **Dovecot** and **sendmail** we need to make some changes in the **/etc/hosts** file.

Assuming that the computer you want to be your mail server has the IP address 192.168.1.100 you'll need to edit the **/etc/hosts** file as follows:

```
# Do not remove the following line, or various programs
# that require network functionality will fail.
127.0.0.1 localhost.localdomain localhost
::1localhost6.localdomain6          localhost6
192.168.1.100 mailserver.home       mailserver
```

Notice that I have added a new line to the already existing ones indicating that your mail server's IP address is 192.168.1.100 and the host name is **mailserver.home**

Of course, you'll have to replace the IP address I used in my example with yours.

Save your settings and go to the next step: install **Dovecot** using a terminal by typing **yum install dovecot** or using **Pirut** by selecting the **Dovecot** package in the Mail Server package group.

The configuration file for Dovecot is **/etc/dovecot.conf.**
Before editing this file I recommend to save it in your computer.
Assuming that you want to use **POP3** or/and **IMAP**, for a basic configuration, all you have to do is to open this file with a text editor and edit it as follows:

- Find the line:

  ```
  #protocols = imap imaps pop3 pop3s
  ```

- Activate it by removing the pound character and choose the protocols you want so it will look like this:

  ```
  protocols = pop3
          or
  protocols = imap
  ```

or
```
protocols = pop3 imap
```

- Save your settings and exit the text editor
- Start **Dovecot** and eventually make sure it will start automatically next time you'll reboot the computer:

  service dovecot start and/or **chkconfig dovecot on**

- Test the connection.
  Knowing that POP3 uses **TCP port 110** and IMAP uses **TCP port 143**, from a terminal type:

  telnet localhost 110 and/or **telnet localhost 143**

After you've configured **Dovecot** you have to configure the **sendmail** service. The **sendmail** service is installed by default in Red Hat® Enterprise Linux® distributions, but you'll also need the **sendmail-cf** package which will be faster installed if from a terminal you type **yum install sendmail-cf.**

Another method to install this package is using **pirut** and then selecting the aforementioned package from the Mail Server package group.

The configuration file for **sendmail** is **/etc/mail/sendmail.cf.**
This file is huge so the easiest way to configure **sendmail** will be through a smaller file that contains only the most relevant directives: **/etc/mail/sendmail.mc.**

A few brief explanations for the files contained in the **/etc/mail** directory are required before editing the **/etc/mail/sendmail.mc** file.
The output of the **ls -l** command for the **/etc/mail** directory should reveal the following:

```
[root@localhost ~]# ls -l /etc/mail
-rw-r--r-- 1 root root   409 Nov 26 15:42 access
-rw-r----- 1 root root 12288 Nov 26 15:42 access.db
-rw-r--r-- 1 root root     0 Mar 14  2007 domaintable
-rw-r----- 1 root root 12288 Nov  2 13:28 domaintable.db
-rw-r--r-- 1 root root  5521 Mar 14  2007 helpfile
-rw-r--r-- 1 root root    64 Mar 14  2007 local-host-names
-rw-r--r-- 1 root root     0 Mar 14  2007 mailertable
-rw-r----- 1 root root 12288 Nov  2 13:28 mailertable.db
```

```
-rw-r--r-- 1 root root  1048 Mar 14  2007 Makefile
-rw-r--r-- 1 root root 58142 Nov 26 15:32 sendmail.cf
-rw-r--r-- 1 root root 58194 Nov  2 13:28 sendmail.cf.bak
-rw-r--r-- 1 root root  7215 Nov 26 15:32 sendmail.mc
-r--r--r-- 1 root root 41275 Mar 14  2007 submit.cf
-rw-r--r-- 1 root root   940 Mar 14  2007 submit.mc
-rw-r--r-- 1 root root   127 Mar 14  2007 trusted-users
-rw-r--r-- 1 root root     0 Mar 14  2007 virtusertable
-rw-r----- 1 root root 12288 Nov  2 13:28 virtusertable.db
```

- **access**   - This file controls the access to your mail server. By default, the access is supported only from the local host. Here you can add networks or host names you want your server to accept or deny connections from.

Examples:

- to allow the **192.168.49.0** domain to connect to your mail server, the line you have to add into this file is:

```
192.168.49                   RELAY
```

- to deny access for this domain with an error message, the entry will be:

```
192.168.49                   REJECT
```

- to deny access without an error message, the entry will be:

```
192.168.49                   DISCARD
```

Notice how I've introduced the domain: there is no dot at the end of the address!
Similar you can insert the name of the domain or the IP address of a certain computer.

- **domaintable**   - The file helps you mapping different domains.

Example:
You changed the name of your domain from **virtual.home** to **example.test**.
In this case a user that had the e-mail address **user@virtual.home** will
receive now messages at **user@example.test.**
But for this to happen you'll need to add in this file the following:

```
virtual.home         example.test
```

Now you're sure that any messages sent by someone to
user@virtual.home will be forwarded to **user@example.test**

- **helpfile**   - This file contains a list of help commands useful when you manage your mail server from the **sendmail** prompt. This can be accessed by typing the **telnet localhost 25** command for non-encrypted transfers, or **telnet localhost 465** command for encrypted transfers.

- **local-host-names**   - Here you can add host names or aliases for you mail server. Each host name and alias must be introduced one per line.

- **mailertable**   - With this file you can manage multiple e-mail domains on the same server. See **http://www.sendmail.org** for detailed information.

- **Makefile**   - Is a script invoked with the **make -C /etc/mail** command necessary to compile the **sendmail. cf** file.

- **sendmail.cf**   - The main **sendmail** configuration file

- **sendmail.mc**   - The macro used to configure the mail server. After you're done editing it, by invoking the **make -C /etc/mail** command, you'll generate a new **sendmail.cf** file.

- **spamassassin**   - Is a directory that contains configuration files for reducing spam. You might not see it in **/etc/mail** if you haven't select the spamassasin rpm package to be installed.

To install it use the **yum install spamassassin** command from a terminal, or **Pirut** and then in the Mail Server group select this package.

To configure **spamassassin** on you local received mail change directory into **/etc/mail/spamassassin** and issue the command **rpm -qi spamassassin.**

The output will instruct you to create a file named **/etc/procmailrc** and to add in it the following entry:

```
INCLUDERC=/etc/mail/spamassassin/spamassassin-default.rc
```

Observation
*In case you want to use **spamassassin** on your system, after you have installed this service and configured it as described don't forget to start it and also make sure it will start any time in case of system reboot.*
For this use the following commands:

service spamassassin start *and/or* **chkconfig spamassassin on**

- **submit.cf**   - The main outgoing **sendmail** configuration file.

- **submit.mc**   - The macro that you can edit and generate a new **submit.cf** file.

- **trusted-users**   - A list of special users that can send e-mails without generating sendmail warnings.

- **virtusertable**   - Supports e-mail forwarding.

- **/etc/aliases**   - Supports e-mail forwarding.

Observation
*Notice that I've introduced here also the **/etc/aliases** file with the same description as for the **virtusertable** file.*
In a certain way both files do the same thing: e-mail forwarding.
In a few examples I'll present how exactly each file influences the functionality of the mail server.

Example 1

Let's say that you want messages sent to **user_a** to be received by **user_b.**
You have to edit the **/etc/aliases** file and introduce a line containing the following:

```
user_a:              user_b
```

After saving the changes in **/etc/aliases** you must run the **newaliases**
command!

Example 2

Your company has a Human Resources department and you want **user_x** and
user_y working in this department to handle the external e-mails received
from an user who's e-mail address is **nick@domain.test.**

The aforementioned Human Resources workers have the following e-mail addresses:
user_x@example.company and **user_y@example.company.**

To solve this problem you'll have to add on your server (if doesn't exist yet)
a new user named **humanresources.**
Obviously the e-mail address for the user **humanresources** will be
humanresources@example.company.

Next step will be to edit the **/etc/mail/virtusertable** as follows:

```
nick@domain.test              humanresources
```

Then you have to edit the **/etc/aliases** file as folows:

```
humanresources:              user_x, user_y
```

What if you want any e-mail coming from any external network to be
received by **user_a** and **user_b ?**

For this you'll have to modify the **/etc/mail/virtusertable** like this:

```
*              humanresources
```

Don't forget to run the **newaliases** command and eventually to edit the
/etc/mail/access file allowing or denying connections to your mail server!

I'll get back to the configuration of the sendmail service and I remind you that it is a good idea to save the **/etc/mail/sendmail.mc** file before editing it.

- Open with a text editor the **/etc/mail/sendmail.mc** file and find the entry :

```
DAEMON_OPTIONS(`Port=smtp,Addr=127.0.0.1, Name=MTA')dnl
```

This line is active by default and says that the **DAEMON_OPTIONS** directive doesn't accept incoming mail from outside your system.
But you want to allow other computers to use your sendmail server!

This can be done in two ways:

a) You can suspend this directive by adding in front of it the **dnl** macro so the entry will be:

```
dnl DAEMON_OPTIONS(`Port=smtp,Addr=127.0.0.1, Name=MTA')dnl
```

b) You can let this directive active but delete the localhost address so the entry will be:

```
DAEMON_OPTIONS(`Port=smtp, Name=MTA')dnl
```

- Find the entry:

```
FEATURE(`accept_unresolvable_domains')dnl
```

Notice that by default it is active (doesn't have the **dnl** macro in front of it !).
I assume that you want to accept unresolvable domains, so for the purpose of this exercise do not add the **dnl** macro in front of it.

- Save your settings and exit the text editor.

- For changes to take effect you must generate a new **sendmail.cf** file. From a terminal type:

  make -C /etc/mail

- Restart your server to make sure it will read the new configuration file and make sure it will start at reboot. From a terminal type:

  service sendmail restart and **chkconfig sendmail on**

- Test your connection knowing that **sendmail** uses **TCP port 25** for non secure communication:

telnet localhost 25

Observation
Don't forget to edit the /etc/mail/access file and insert the domains or the IP addresses you want your mail server to accept connections from!

Time to check your work!

Go to another computer (virtual machine) in your network, open and edit the **/etc/hosts** file on that machine so it will look like this:

```
# Do not remove the following line, or various programs
# that require network functionality will fail.
127.0.0.1          localhost.localdomain          localhost
::1                localhost6.localdomain6        localhost6
192.168.1.101      virtual.home                   virtual
192.168.1.100      mailserver.home                mailserver
```

As you can see in the **/etc/hosts** file of the machine you use to test the mail server, I introduced two new entries:

- the IP address (192.168.1.101) and the host name (virtual.home) of your test machine.
- the IP address (192.168.1.100) and the hostname (mailserver.home) of your mail server.

The IP's and host names presented were just examples. You have to use your own IP's and host names.
Review Chapter 5 to remember how to change the host name and domain for your computer.

From the test machine, open a terminal and type:

echo "test" | mail root@mailserver.home

The command will send an e-mail to your server containing the word **test.** You can check the **/var/log/maillog** file on the test machine to see how your e-mail was handled.

If everything was configured correctly **root** on your mail server should receive the e-mail.

Using the command line application mail

Sending an e-mail to an user it's easy. All you have to do is to open a terminal and type: **mail user_name@host_name.domain_name.**

For example :
mail nick@example.test
You'll be prompted to introduce the subject of your e-mail:

Subject: This is a test

By pressing **Enter** you can start on the next line to type your message for the specified user.
When you're done composing you mail press **Enter** again and then press **Ctrl+D.**
This time you'll be prompted to complete the field **Cc** in case you want to send the same message to other users.
To send you message press **Enter**.

Reading messages is done issuing from a terminal the same command **mail**. If any e-mail is in your mailbox, the command will display a list with new messages and read messages.
All messages are numbered, so to read a certain message all you have to do is to introduce the specific number of the desired message.

To delete a message press **d** or **dn** where **n** is the number of the message you want to delete.
Deleting multiple messages is done if you press **d1-n.**
This will delete all messages from **1** to **n.**
After you're done reading and/or deleting messages, by pressing **q** and then **Enter** you'll exit the **mail** application.

This is the easiest and fastest way to check your work.
But there is also the other method implying the graphical application called **Email** that you have to configure on the test machine.
I encourage you to practice both methods so, in the end, you'll decide which one was faster.

Using POP3S and IMAPS in Dovecot

Assuming that you want to enable the secure versions of **POP3** and/or **IMAP** protocols, there are a few more steps for a basic configuration of such server.

Open with a text editor the **/etc/dovecot.conf** file.

- Establish which secure protocols you want to enable:

```
protocols = pop3s
        or
protocols = imaps
        or
protocols = pop3s imaps
```

- Find the entry #ssl_disable = no and activate it:

```
ssl_disable = no
```

- You'll have to tell the server where the secure certificates are stored. For that, find the entries:

```
#ssl_cert_file = /etc/pki/dovecot/certs/dovecot.pem
#ssl_key_file = /etc/pki/dovecot/private/dovecot.pem
```
Activate them by removing the pound character from in front of them:

```
ssl_cert_file = /etc/pki/dovecot/certs/dovecot.pem
ssl_key_file = /etc/pki/dovecot/private/dovecot.pem
```

- Save settings and exit the text editor

- Change directory into **/etc/pki/dovecot/** and fill in the **dovecot-openssl.cnf** file with the correct values.

- Next step will be removing the certificates from both **/etc/pki/dovecot/certs** and **/etc/pki/dovecot/private** directories.

  rm /etc/pki/dovecot/certs/dovecot.pem
  and
  rm /etc/pki/dovecot/private/dovecot.pem

- Change directory into **/etc/pki/dovecot** and generate new certificates calling from this directory the following script:

  /usr/share/doc/dovecot-[version_number]/examples/mkcert.sh

  From a terminal type:

  cd /etc/pki/dovecot
  /usr/share/doc/dovecot-[version_number]/examples/mkcert.sh

- Start or restart **Dovecot** also making sure that next time when you'll reboot your computer the service will start automatically:

  service dovecot start or **service dovecot restart**
  chkconfig dovecot on

- Knowing that POP3S uses **TCP port 995** and IMAPS uses **TCP port 993**, test the connection by typing from a terminal:

  telnet localhost 995 and/or **telnet localhost 993**

Using SSL (secure sockets layer) encryption in sendmail

You can configure sendmail to encrypt incoming and outgoing e-mails using SSL. In what follows I'll describe how to generate a self-signed certificate and how to make sendmail use it.

- Open a terminal and change directory into **/etc/pki/tls/certs**

  cd /etc/pki/tls/certs

- Execute the following command:

  make sendmail.pem

The script will generate the certificates and it will prompt to type in specific information.

After generating the certificates you must edit the **/etc/mail/sendmail.mc** file as follows:

- Open with a text editor the **/etc/mail/sednmail.mc** file and find the following entry:

```
dnl DAEMON_OPTIONS(`Port=smtps, Name=TLSMTA, M=s')dnl
```

Activate it by removing the **dnl** macro so it will look like :

```
DAEMON_OPTIONS(`Port=smtps, Name=TLSMTA, M=s')dnl
```

- Find the entries referring to how SSL handles the new generated certificate and activate them so they will look like this:

```
define(`confCACERT_PATH', `/etc/pki/tls/certs')dnl
define(`confCACERT', `/etc/pki/tls/certs/ca-bundle.crt')dnl
define(`confSERVER_CERT', `/etc/pki/tls/certs/sendmail.pem')dnl
define(`confSERVER_KEY', `/etc/pki/tls/certs/sendmail.pem')dnl
```

- If you want the sendmail server to accept incoming e-mail from outside your network, don't forget to edit the following line as I have explained previously:

```
dnl DAEMON_OPTIONS(`Port=smtp,Addr=127.0.0.1, Name=MTA')dnl
```

or

```
DAEMON_OPTIONS(`Port=smtp, Name=MTA')dnl
```

- Save your settings and exit the text editor.

- Generate a new **sendmail.cf** file by issuing the following command:

make -C /etc/mail

- Restart your server for the changes to take efect.

service sendmail restart

- Test the connection knowing that **sendmail** uses **TCP port 465** for encrypted communication.
  From a terminal type:

telnet localhost 465

Observation

*Be very careful when you edit the **/etc/mail/sendmail.mc** file: check to have no extra blank spaces between the entries, or characters missing in the expressions that define **DAEMON_OPTIONS** or **FEATURES**.*

*Sendmail uses the **/var/log/maillog** file to write log entries.*
In case something goes wrong check messages in this file.

Chapter 9.   SSH, NTP and XINETD

SSH (Secure Shell) server configuration

The **ssh** RPM package is installed by default in any Red Hat® Enterprise Linux® based distribution and contains in the **/etc/ssh/** directory all necessary files for configuring your computer as a SSH server and/or as a SSH client.

This service needs the **sshd** daemon up and running to insure it's functionality.
The **sshd** daemon listens by default on **TCP port 22** allowing encrypted communication between computers.
Encryption is based on generating a pair of keys consisting in a private encryption key (kept secret on your computer) and a public encryption key.

How sending-receiving encrypted data works?

Let's say **A** (sender) wants to send a message to **B** (known recipient).
The sender will look for recipient's public key and use it to encrypt the message about to be sent.

At the other end the recipient needs to read the just arrived encrypted message. For this, recipient's secret private key will be used to unscramble the message and make it readable.

If **A** wants to authenticate the message then, through a mathematical algorithm which involves the sender's private key and the message itself is obtained the so called digital signature of the message.
The message having the digital signature attached is send to the recipient.

To verify the signature of the message (confirming that the message is authentic), the recipient will use a procedure that involves this time the message, the signature and the sender's public key.

In the following example I'll describe how you can use the public and private keys to **ssh** a server from a client computer through regular users:

You want a regular user named **check** on the machine named **virtual.home.test** to **ssh** a regular user named **local** on your server named **myserver.home.test**

- Login as regular user **check** on the client computer (**virtual.home.test**) and generate the pair of keys you want:

    - to generate a **DSA** pair of keys use the following command from a terminal:

      ssh-keygen -t dsa

    - to generate a **RSA** pair use this command:

      ssh-keygen -t rsa

    - to generate a **RSA1** pair the command will be:

      ssh-keygen -t rsa1

While any type of keys are generated you'll be prompted to a dialog similar to this:

```
Enter file in which to save the key
(/home/check/.ssh/[private_key_file]):
Enter passphrase (empty for no passphrase):
Enter same passphrase again:
Your identification has been saved in
/home/check/.ssh/[private_key_file]
Your public key has been saved in
/home/check/.ssh/[public_key_file]
The key fingerprint is:
a3:00:03:9d:9f:8f:5d:88:e0:bf:d5:06:24:20:c0:42
check@virtual.home.test
```

It is a good idea to protect your private key with a passphrase so, insert a passphrase when prompted. This way you'll increase security of the communication between your computers..

The [private_key_file] and [public_key_file] files will be in this case the names of the files where will be written the private encryption key respective the public encryption key.

After the keys were generated go to the computer that you want to prepare to be a SSH server (in my example **myserver.home.test**), login as regular user **local** and create in **/home/local** a hidden directory named **.ssh**:

> **mkdir /home/local/.ssh**

- In the new **/home/local.ssh** directory, you must create now a file named **authorized_keys**

> **touch /home/local/.ssh/authorized_keys**

It is very important to establish the following permissions for the **/home/local/.ssh** directory and for the **/home/local/.ssh/authorized_keys** file:

> **chmod 700 /home/local/.ssh**
> **chmod 600 /home/local/.ssh/authorized_keys**

While you're still logged in as regular user **local** on the SSH server, with what the **/etc/ssh/sshd_config** file provides by default (remember that I did not operate any modification yet in this file) you can now use the **sftp** command to bring any generated public key from the client computer (**virtual.home.test**) into the home directory of the regular user **local** on the server computer (**myserver.home.test**):

> **sftp check@virtual.home.test**

The command will bring the sftp> prompt and from here you can retrieve any public key generated before in this example.
Remember that for any generated type of keys you'll use, the name of the public key will end with **.pub**

> **sftp get id_dsa.pub**
> or
> **sftp get id_rsa.pub**
> or
> **sftp get identity.pub**

Any of these commands will bring the desired public key into the **/home/local** directory.

You can also log in as **root** and use the **scp** command to bring the private key from **check's** home directory (remember it is in **/home/check/.ssh/** [type_of_key].pub) in the server.

Regardless the method you choose to bring the public key generated by user **check** into the computer that will be your SSH server, you must copy it into the **/home/local/.ssh/authorized_keys** file.

After you've done all of this, now you can edit the **/etc/ssh/sshd_config** activating and changing options to obtain a minimal configuration for your SSH server that will permit authentication based on private-public pair of keys. The minimal changes I've done for this example will be like this:

```
Port 22
Protocol 2
PermitRootLogin no
PubkeyAuthentication yes
AuthorizedKeysFile      .ssh/authorized_keys
PasswordAuthentication no
ChallengeResponseAuthentication no
GSSAPIAuthentication no
GSSAPICleanupCredentials yes

UsePAM yes

# Accept locale-related environment variables
AcceptEnv LANG LC_CTYPE LC_NUMERIC LC_TIME LC_COLLATE LC_
MONETARY LC_MESSAGES
AcceptEnv LC_PAPER LC_NAME LC_ADDRESS LC_TELEPHONE LC_
MEASUREMENT
AcceptEnv LC_IDENTIFICATION LC_ALL

X11Forwarding yes
Subsystem       sftp    /usr/libexec/openssh/sftp-server
```

Observation:
*This configuration refers to **Protocol 2** which applies in case you want to use **DSA** or **RSA** keys.*

A similar configuration for **/etc/ssh/sshd_config** file can be used in case you want to generate **RSA1** keys but the difference will be that instead of the entries `Protocol 2` and `PubkeyAuthentication yes` you must use `Protocol 1` and `RSAAuthentication yes`

After you have prepared the SSH server and operated any modifications in server's main configuration file restart the service by typing from a terminal the following command:

service sshd restart

Go to the client machine (in my example **virtual.home.test**), login as user **check** and try to ssh user **local** on the server (**myserver.home.test**) by typing from a terminal :

ssh local@myserver.home.test

If you don't have a qualified domain name for your machines in your network you can use the IP addresses of the machines instead :

ssh local@192.168.1.100

Replace the IP address I used with the IP address of your SSH server. You should be able to gain access to **local's** home directory on the server without being asked for a password any time you use **ssh** command.

A good setting is not to permit **root** users to login into your SSH server. Notice that I've done this by activating and editing the appropriate entry like this:

```
PermitRootLogin no
```

You can also allow or deny only certain users to login into your server. Do this by specifying their names separated by spaces when you activate the desired option `AllowUsers` and/or `DenyUsers`.

For example, allow only user **local** to access your **SSH server :**

```
AllowUsers local
```

By activating the entry `X11Forwarding yes` you can login from a remote machine into your SSH server gaining access to any GUI tool.

The client's configuration file is **/etc/ssh/ssh_config** file.
If you want your client to have access to any GUI tool on the server, you'll have to edit and activate the entry `ForwardX11 yes` and on the server machine you must edit and activate in the **/etc/ssh/sshd_config** file the entry `X11Forwarding yes`.

Please read the manual (**man sshd_config** and **man ssh_config**) to obtain all necessary information about the options in these files and how any of them will affect the functionality of your server-client machines.

A graphical tool is also available in case you don't want to use the terminal to ssh your machines.

On the client machine go to **Places** and click on **Connect to Server.**

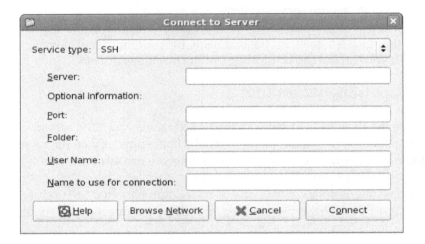

From the **Service type** select what service do you want to use to connect to your machine (in this case ssh or sftp), then insert the IP address for **Server** and 22 for **Port** (if you want to use the default TCP port 22).
Click on **Connect** and in the next box fill in the user name and the password for the user (in this example it is **local**) on the server.

NTP (Network Time Protocol) Server configuration

Time synchronization between servers around the world is very important. Just think about different transactions taking place on line in real life where time is crucial !

I'll explain the steps you'll have to take for configuring a NTP server for your local network and how client computers will connect to your server.

The configuration file for the NTP server is located in **/etc/ntp.conf** and you'll need the **ntpd** service up and running for a full functional server.

I suggest you to deactivate for now the Firewall and SELinux services.

Assuming that you're practicing this server configuration on virtual machines prepare one of them to be the NTP server for your network:

- Open with a text editor the **/etc/ntp.conf** file and edit the following entries:

  ```
  restrict default kod nomodify notrap
  ```

- Activate and modify using your IP addresses the following entry:

  ```
  # Hosts on local network are less restricted.
  restrict 192.168.1.0 mask 255.255.255.0 nomodify notrap
  ```

The first entry you've just modified specifies default restrictions for Ipv4. I considered for this exercise that you are working only with private Ipv4 address classes so all entries referring to Ipv6 address classes were eliminated.

The `kod` option prevents the so called **Kiss Of Death** that might bring down your NTP server in case of attack.

The options `nomodify` and `notrap` prevents other NTP servers to modify this server respectively denies the message trap service.

In the next step I have added the local network specifying it's IP address and subnet mask with the same options `nomodify` and `notrap`.
Use the IP address of your own local network for this step.

Start or restart your NTP server by issuing from a terminal the following commands:

service ntpd start or **service ntpd restart**

You will also want your NTP server to start automatically every time you'll reboot the computer so use the **chkconfig ntpd on** command to do this.

Go to a computer that you want to be a client for your configured NTP server and use one of these two methods to connect to it:

1. Open a terminal on the client and type **system-config-time**, or go to **System** choose **Administration** and then click on **Date and Time**, or just right click on the clock displayed on the right corner of your Desktop.
Regardless how you'll do it, in the end, by selecting the **Network Time Protocol** tab you'll see the following dialog box:

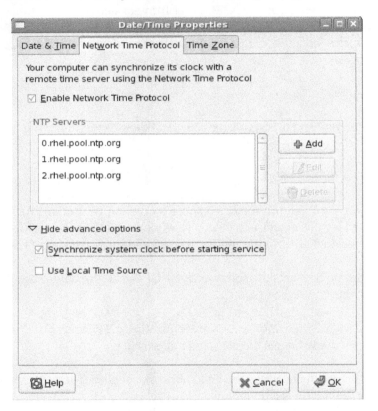

Now you can press the **Add** button and this will help you introduce in client's **/etc/ntp.conf** file the IP address of your NTP server.

When you're done, just check the box **Synchronize system clock before starting service** and then press **OK.**
This will start synchronization of the client computer with your server.

2. Open with a text editor client's **/etc/ntp.conf** file and manually add in this file the following two entries:

```
server 192.168.1.100
restrict 192.168.1.100 mask 255.255.255.255 nomodify notrap
noquery
```

I assumed that the IP address of your NTP server is 192.168.1.100. You'll have to replace it according to your network.

If you don't want your client computer to search other NTP servers you can edit it's **/etc/ntp.conf** file and suspend all entries that specify remote NTP servers:

```
# Use public servers from the pool.ntp.org project.
# Please consider joining the pool
#(http://www.pool.ntp.org/join.html).
#server 0.rhel.pool.ntp.org
#server 1.rhel.pool.ntp.org
#server 2.rhel.pool.ntp.org
```

The same thing is done if you use the graphical tool by selecting each entry referring to NTP servers and pressing successively the **Delete** button. Unfortunately this will remove these entries for good so, the best way to practice in this case is editing the client's **/etc/ntp.conf** file and add the pound character in front of the aforementioned entries.

After you have operated the modifications in client's **/etc/ntp.conf** file you'll have to restart the client computer.

When restart is done open a terminal on the client computer and issue the following command:

ntpdate -u 192.168.1.100

If everything was configured correct you should see a response similar with this:

```
9  Sep   19:17:35  ntpdate[9784]:adjust  time
server  192.168.1.100  offset  -0.019273  sec
```

Then, to verify if your client is synchronized with your NTP server type :

ntpq -p

You'll get a response similar to this:

```
remote        refid        st t when poll reach delay offset jitter
=====================================================================
192.168.1.100 198.38.16.1 3 u 223   256  377   0.95  1.282 13.26
```

As long as for **offset** and **jitter** you'll have values different from zero, the client is synchronized with your NTP server.

The Extended Internet Services Daemon (XINETD)

The **xinetd** also known as Internet Super Server operates services that don't have their own daemons.
There is a list of files in **/etc/xinetd.d** directory and each file present here defines specific parameters for services controlled by **xinetd**.

On the other hand **xinetd** has it's generic configuration file in **/etc/xinetd.conf.**

Let's take a look at this file first.
Right from the beginning this file informs you that "Settings in the default section will be inherited by all service configurations unless explicitly overridden in the service configuration"

Then follows the defaults section where you can see a list of parameters (some not activated and some activated and having already default values established) related to the "general behavior" of any service listed in **/etc/xinetd.d** directory that you want to be active (running).

I will present only how you can enable/disable a service that needs **xinetd.**

As an example I'll use **krb5-telnet**, a service listed with a configuration file in **/etc/xinetd.d** directory.

I assume you want this service up and running on a computer that has the IP address 192.168.1.100 and also you want this service to be accessed only from computers in your private network (in this example the IP address of your network will be 192.168.1.0/24).

For a basic configuration you have to open with a text editor the specific configuration file for the aforementioned service – in this case the **/etc/xinetd/krb5-telnet** file.
The file will show the following:

```
# default: off
# description: The kerberized telnet server accepts normal telnet
# sessions, but can also use Kerberos 5 authentication.
service telnet
{
        flags            = REUSE
        socket_type      = stream
        wait             = no
        user             = root
        server           = /usr/kerberos/sbin/telnetd
        log_on_failure  += USERID
        disable          = yes
}
```

Notice that this service is disabled by default (disable = yes).
To enable the service, you have to change this entry to disable = no
Save your settings and exit the text editor.

Now, open with a text editor the **/etc/xinetd.conf** file and change some generic parameters here.
For example, you could establish in this file the following :

```
only_from = 192.168.1.100
only_from = 192.168.1.111
no_access = 192.168.1.112
```

Using only_from option and specifying for it two IP addresses as shown, I have allowed the **telnet** service to be used only from the computers with the aforementioned IP addresses while any user from the computer with the IP address 192.168.1.112 will not be able to login via **telnet** (notice that also option no_access is active and specifys the IP address).

Observation
Think that using and defining values for `only_from` *and* `no_access` *options is like using TCP Wrappers.*
If for services that are running their own daemon you can edit the
/etc/hosts.allow and /etc/hosts.deny by specifying certain services to accept or deny connections from, same thing is obtained here when it's about services governed by the Extended Internet Service Daemon.
The use of TCP Wrappers will be explained later in this book.
When time will come just remember this analogy.

A faster way to have the **krb3-telnet** service up and running would be using the **chkconfig** command:

chkconfig krb5-telnet on

This command will automatically turn the option `disable = no` in the **/etc/xinetd.d/kreb5-telnet** file.

Once used this command it will turn on this service every time you'll start your computer so remember to turn the service off after you're done with this exercise by typing **chkconfig krb5-telnet off**.
The manual (man xinetd.conf, man xinetd) provides detailed information about all settings available to configure **xinetd** so don't forget to consult it!

Chapter 10. Domain Name Service – DNS

The DNS service maintains a database that translates IP addresses into domain names and vice-versa.

When searching for a domain, instead of introducing the IP address you will introduce the name of the domain and the DNS service will search for the associated IP address if exists.

The commonly used DNS service is BIND (Berkley Internet Name Service) based on the functionality of it's daemon **named.**

First you'll need to install the necessary packages using **yum install bind*** or using the graphical package manager by selecting **Servers** and then **DNS Name Server.**

For Red Hat® Enterprise Linux® based distributions this will install the following packages:

> bind
> bind-chroot
> bind-devel
> bind-libbind-devel
> bind-libs
> bind-sdb
> bind-utils

There are four DNS servers that I will describe through examples in this chapter:

- **caching-only DNS server** – stores answers of recent requests in cache and when the server receives a query it will offer the answer from it's cache if, of course, has an answer. If not, it will forward the query to the next DNS server on the network.

- **forwarding-only DNS server** – forwards all requests to another DNS server.

- **slave DNS server** – receives data from a master DNS server.

- **master DNS server** – is an authoritative server that stores records for a domain.

Configuring a caching-only name server

If you want to configure this type of server you need to install one more package besides the packages I have mentioned: the **caching-nameserver** package.

    yum install caching-nameserver

Now that all necessary packages are installed you need to create the configuration file **named.conf** in the **/var/named/chroot/etc directory.**

- **cd /var/named/chroot/etc**

- **touch named.conf**

- Copy the content of **/var/named/chroot/etc/named.caching-nameserver.conf** file into the new created **/var/named/chroot/etc/named.conf** file. Assuming that you are already in the **/var/named/chroot/etc** directory, the command will be :

  cat named.caching-nameserver.conf > named.conf

- Open with a text editor the **/var/named/chroot/etc/named.conf** file. It will look something like this:

```
options {
        listen-on port 53 { 127.0.0.1; };
        listen-on-v6 port 53 { ::1; };
        directory      "/var/named";
        dump-file      "/var/named/data/cache_dump.db";
        statistics-file "/var/named/data/named_stats.txt";
        memstatistics-file
"/var/named/data/named_mem_stats.txt";
```

```
        // Those options should be used carefully because
        they disable
        //port randomization
        // query-source     port 53;
        // query-source-v6 port 53;
allow-query      { localhost; };
};
logging {
        channel default_debug {
                file "data/named.run";
                severity dynamic;
        };
};
view localhost_resolver {
        match-clients          { localhost; };
        match-destinations { localhost; };
        recursion yes;
        include "/etc/named.rfc1912.zones";
};
```

- The first two directives specify the TCP/IP communication port number 53 for both IPv4 and IPv6.
  Assuming that the IP address of your computer is 192.168.1.100 edit the listen-on port 53 { 127.0.0.1; }; directive so it will look like this:

```
listen-on port 53 { 127.0.0.1; 192.168.1.100; };
```

Be careful when you edit this file so no extra spaces will interfere and also don't forget the necessary semicolons!

- The directive allow-query { localhost; }; specifies the IP addresses allowed to get information from this server. To extend this to your local network, assuming that your network address is 192.168.1.0/24 the entry will be modified like this:

```
allow-query { localhost; 192.168.1.0/24; };
```

I remind you that I have use the IP address 192.168.1.100 as an example. Replace it with the IP address of your computer.

- Save settings and exit.

- The file **/var/named/chroot/etc/named.conf** is configured but it has to be linked to the **/etc/named.conf** file:

      cd /etc
      ln -s /var/named/chroot//etc/named.conf named.conf

If you list the **/etc** directory, besides the new symlink created
`(named.conf -> /var/named/chroot//etc/named.conf)` you can see
there another two BIND configuration files linked similar :

```
named.caching-nameserver.conf ->
/var/named/chroot//etc/named.caching-nameserver.conf

named.rfc1912.zones -> /var/named/chroot//etc/named.rfc1912.zones
```

- Open with a text editor the **/etc/hosts** file and add here an entry that maps the name of your computer to the IP address of your network card:

```
# Do not remove the following line, or various programs
# that require network functionality will fail.
127.0.0.1          localhost.localdomain     localhost
::1                localhost6.localdomain6   localhost6
192.168.1.100      localhost.localdomain     localhost
```

- Save this settings and exit the text editor.

You need to tell the local resolver what DNS server to search for.
This will be done by editing the **/etc/resolv.conf** file.

- Open with a text editor the **/etc/resolv.conf** file, remove all entries there and add the following new directives:

```
search 192.168.1.100
nameserver 192.168.1.100
```

Replace the IP address I have used here as an example with the IP address of your computer.

To prevent overwriting your settings in case of restart edit the
/etc/sysconfig/network-scripts/ifcfg-eth0 file and add the entry `PEERDNS=no`
so in the end it will look similar to this:

```
DEVICE=eth0
BOOTPROTO=dhcp
HWADDR=00:0A:09:B6:96:2F
ONBOOT=yes
PEERDNS=no
```

Start your **caching-only name server** and eventually make it start
automatically in case of reboot :

- **service named start** and/or **chkconfig named on**

To test your work fast you can use the **dig** command.
From a terminal type for example **dig www.google.com** and notice the
response for `Query time` and `SERVER`.

For `Query time` you will see an answer in milliseconds and for `SERVER` you
should see the IP address of your computer.
According to the example I have used it should be:

```
SERVER:192.168.1.100#53(192.168.1.100)
```

Use again **dig www.google.com** and this time notice the `Query time`.
Now it should display a very low value in milliseconds.
This indicates that your **caching-only server** saved the information in it's
cache and when you have used for the second time the **dig** command, the
information was served from the server's cache.

Configuring a master DNS server

I will use an exercise as an example for configuring a master DNS server.
First make sure that Firewall and SELinux are not activated for this exercise.

Exercise:
Configure a computer named **myserver** to be a DNS server for two
computers on you internal network : **virtual1** and **virtual2**

The domain for your internal network is **home.test.**
The IP address of your network is 192.168.1.0/24
The IP address of the DNS server is 192.168.1.100, the computer named **virtual1** has the IP address 192.168.1.111 and the computer named **virtual2** has the IP address 192.168.1.112

- Check the existence of the following packages on your computer:
  bind
  bind-chroot
  bind-devel
  bind-libbind-devel
  bind-libs
  bind-sdb
  bind-utils
  caching-nameserver

  From a terminal type the following commands:

  rpm -qa | grep bind*
       and
  rpm -qa | grep chaching*

If you did not configure yet the **caching-only name server** as I have described earlier in this chapter, you will have to install all aforementioned packages:

Use yum for installing as follows:

> **yum install bind***
> **yum install chaching-nameserver**

- Create the **named.conf** file in the **/var/named/chroot/etc**

  cd /var/named/chroot/etc
  touch named.conf

- Copy the content of **/var/named/chroot/etc/named.caching-nameserver.conf** file into the new created **/var/named/chroot/etc/named.conf** file.

  cat named.caching-nameserver.conf > named.conf

- Open with a text editor the **/var/named/chroot/etc/named.conf** file and edit it to look like this:

```
options {
    listen-on port 53 { 127.0.0.1; 192.168.1.100; };
    listen-on-v6 port 53 { ::1; };
    directory      "/var/named";
    dump-file      "/var/named/data/cache_dump.db";
    statistics-file "/var/named/data/named_stats.txt";
    memstatistics-file "/var/named/data/named_mem_stats.txt";
    query-source       port 53;
    query-source-v6    port 53;

    allow-query      { localhost; 192.168.1.0/24; };
    };
    logging {
        channel default_debug {
            file "data/named.run";
            severity dynamic;
        };
    };

    zone "home.test" IN {
        type master;
        file "home.test.zone";
    };

    zone "1.168.192.in-addr.arpa" IN {
        type master;
        file "home.test.rev.zone";
    };

    include "/etc/rndc.key";
```

Notice that in the "options" section I have underlined the directives that you'll have to enable and configure according to the requirements of this exercise.

In the "`zone`" section you can see that I have added only two zones as needed for this exercise:

- the forward zone section

```
zone "home.test" IN {
        type master;
        file "home.test.zone";
};
```

- the reverse zone section

```
zone "1.168.192.in-addr.arpa" IN {
        type master;
        file "home.test.rev.zone";
};
```

Notice how I've added the IP address of the network (192.168.1.0/24) in the reverse zone: instead of `192.168.1.0` it must be `1.168.192`

For the forward zone, the information is in a file named **home.test.zone** and for the reverse zone the information is in the file named **home.test.rev.zone.**

Another directive I added is `include "/etc/rndc.key";`

- Save settings and exit the text editor

- Change directory into /etc and create a symbolic link of the **/var/named/chroot/etc/named.conf** file in the **/etc** directory:

  cd /etc
  ln -s /var/named/chtoot//etc/named.conf named.conf

- Generate an RNDC (Remote Name Daemon Control) key and include it in the **/etc/rndc.key file.**
  From a terminal issue this command:

  rndc-confgen

After the key was generated you can include in the **/etc/rndc.key** file a **512 bit** encryption key with the following command :

  rndc-confgen -a -b 512

Next step will be creating the **home.test.zone** and **home.test.rev.zone** files and adding the necessary information in both of them.

- Create the **home.test.zone** in the **/var/named/chroot/var/named** directory

  cd /var/named/chroot/var/named
  touch home.test.zone

- Open with a text editor the new created **home.test.zone** file and add in it the following information:

```
$TTL        86400
@           IN   SOA myserver.home.test. root.myserver.home.test. (
                                        2009081100 ; Serial
                                        28800      ; Refresh
                                        14400      ; Retry
                                        3600000    ; Expire
                                        86400 )    ; Minimum
            IN   NS    myserver.home.test.
myserver    IN   A     192.168.1.100
virtual1    IN   A     192.168.1.111
virtual2    IN   A     192.168.1.112
```

The file constructed this way contains some notations:

`$TTL   86400`   - **Time To Live** expressed in seconds for data on your DNS server (default 86400 seconds = 3 days). It is also accepted the syntax **$TTL   3D**

SOA   - **Start Of Authority** describes the zone where it comes from (the computer named **myserver.home.test**), the e-mail of the administrator of this DNS server (**root@ myserver.home.test**) and the following parameters:

- `Serial` number – obtained from a combination of the date this server was created (20090811 = 11th of August 2009) and two digits representing the version number (00 = first created database). Every time you make changes in SOA record the version number *has to be incremented* (01, 02, 03, etc)

- `Refresh` – indicates the period of time after which the master DNS server notifies slave servers to refresh the record (in this example 28800 seconds = 8 hours, also accepted `8H`).

- `Retry` – in case of refresh failure this is the time interval after which slaves DNS servers should wait until trying to refresh again (in this example 14400 = **4H**).

- `Expire` – this has effect only for slave servers and represents the period of time the slave servers have to wait in case they can't reach the master DNS before considering stop querying the master server.

It is a good idea to establish this time interval to be 1 week or 2 weeks. Just in case something happens to your master DNS server, the slave DNS servers will keep serving records for a week or two before they give up. This will give you enough time to solve the problem with your DNS server.

- `Minumum` – represents the minimum time period the DNS slave servers should keep records in their cache.

`NS` = Nameserver   - indicates the name of the server that provides domain name service. In this case **myserver.home.test**

`A` = IPv4 Address   - links a domain name to the IP address of a computer.

- Save your settings and exit the text editor.

- Create a symbolic link of the **/var/named/chroot/var/named/home.test.zone** file in the **/var/named** directory.
  cd /var/named
  ln -s /var/named/chroot//var/named/home.test.zone home.test.zone

- You have to create now the reverse **home.test.rev.zone** file in the **/var/named/chroot/var/named** directory.

  cd /var/named/chroot/var/named
  touch home.test.rev.zone

- Open with a text editor the new created reverse **home.test.rev.zone** file and edit it to look like this:

```
$TTL            86400
@               IN  SOA myserver.home.test. root.myserver.home.test. (
                                        2009081100 ; Serial
                                        28800      ; Refresh
                                        14400      ; Retry
                                        3600000    ; Expire
                                        86400 )    ; Minimum


                IN  NS   myserver.home.test.
100             IN  PTR  myserver.home.test.
111             IN  PTR  virtual1.home.test.
112             IN  PTR  virtual2.home.test.
```

In this file a new element appeared: PTR = Pointer.

The **Pointer** (PTR) in the reverse zone file is the equivalent of the **Ipv4 Address** (A) in the forward zone file only that this time it links the IP address of a computer to a domain name.

- Save settings and exit the text editor.

- Create a symbolic link of the **/var/named/chroot/var/named/home. test.rev.zone** file in the **/var/named** directory:

  cd /var/named
  ln -s /var/named/chroot//var/named/home.test.rev.zone home.test.rev.zone

- Open with a text editor the **/etc/hosts** file of your DNS server and edit it to look like this:

```
# Do not remove the following line, or various programs
# that require network functionality will fail.
127.0.0.1       localhost.localdomain   localhost
::1             localhost6.localdomain6         localhost6
192.168.1.100   myserver.home.test              myserver
```

- Save settings and exit the text editor.

- Establish for your server the host name and the domain name. You can do this by using the command:

hostname myserver

Remember that if you want to make this change permanently you'll have to open with a text editor the **/etc/sysconfig/network** file and edit the entry
```
HOSTNAME=myserver
```

- If your IP address is acquired via DHCP then you'll have to add in the **/etc/sysconfig/network-scripts/ifcfg-et0** file an entry that will prevent overriding the information in **/etc/resolv.conf** file.
  Open the **/etc/sysconfig/network-scripts/ifcfg-et0** file with a text editor and add the PEERDNS=no instruction so in the end you'll obtain something similar to this:

```
DEVICE=eth0
BOOTPROTO=dhcp
HWADDR=00:0A:09:B6:96:2F
ONBOOT=yes
PEERDNS=no
```

- Save settings and exit text editor
- Edit the **/etc/resolv.conf** file and make it look like this:

```
search          home.test
Nameserver      192.168.1.100
```

Finally, it's time to start the server.
From a terminal type:

service named start and **chkconfig named on**

Use **host** and **dig** commands to test your work.
When from a terminal you type **host -l home.test** you should have an answer like this:

```
home.test name server myserver.home.test
myserver.home.test has address 192.168.1.100
virtual1.home.test has address 192.168.1.111
virtual2.home.test has address 192.168.1.112
```

Then type **dig virtual1.home.test** and the answer should be :

```
; <<>> DiG 9.3.4-P1 <<>> virtual1.home.test
;; global options:  printcmd
;; Got answer:
;; ->>HEADER<<- opcode: QUERY, status: NOERROR, id: 27294
;; flags: qr aa rd ra; QUERY: 1, ANSWER: 1, AUTHORITY: 1,
ADDITIONAL: 1

;; QUESTION SECTION:
;virtual1.home.test.            IN      A

;; ANSWER SECTION:
virtual1.home.test.  86400   IN      A        192.168.1.111

;; AUTHORITY SECTION:
home.test.           86400   IN      NS       myserver.home.test.

;; ADDITIONAL SECTION:
virtual2.home.test.  86400   IN      A        192.168.1.112

;; Query time: 3 msec
;; SERVER: 192.168.1.100#53(192.168.1.100)
;; WHEN: Sat Aug 08 16:41:12 2009
;; MSG SIZE  rcvd: 94
```

Issue again the same command but this time for the computer named
virtual2.home.test and observe the returned answer.

You can use the same commands from the client computers **virtual1** and
virtual2 but don't forget to edit the **/etc/hosts** and **/etc/resolv.conf** files for
both clients by adding the appropriate entries.
Also you might need to insert in the **/etc/sysconfig/network-scripts/ifcfg-eth0**
file for both clients, the PEERDNS=no directive.

Observations
*You can extend the requirements of the previous exercise by adding to your
domain a mail server (mail), a Web server and a FTP server.
In this case all you have to do is to modify the forward zone file and the
reverse zone file.*

*Of course this will work for real only if the aforementioned servers were
already configured and you have a **FQDN** (Fully Qualified Domain Name).
Based on this fact the **home.test.zone** file will look like this :*

```
$TTL            86400
@               IN   SOA myserver.home.test. root.myserver.home.test. (
                                            2009081100 ; Serial
                                            28800        ; Refresh
                                            14400        ; Retry
                                            3600000      ; Expire
                                            86400 )      ; Minimum
                IN   NS          myserver.home.test.
myserver        IN   A           192.168.1.100
                IN   MX    10    mail.home.test.
mail            IN   A           192.168.1.100
www             IN   CNAME       myserver
ftp             IN   CNAME       myserver
virtual1        IN   A           192.168.1.111
virtual2        IN   A           192.168.1.112
```

You have notice two new elements in this file:
MX *represents **Mail Exchange** record and deals with the e-mail information
on this server.*
Associated with the MX *record we find a number (in this example –* 10*) that
specifies priority.*
*You can have multiple mail services on your DNS server so you'll need to
specify a priority for each one of them.*
A lower number means a higher priority.
CNAME *means **Canonical Name** and links an alias to a domain name.*

*The **home.test.rev.zone** file will look like this:*

```
$TTL            86400
@               IN   SOA myserver.home.test. root.myserver.home.test. (
                                            2009081100 ; Serial
                                            28800        ; Refresh
                                            14400        ; Retry
                                            3600000      ; Expire
                                            86400 )      ; Minimum
                IN   NS          myserver.home.test.
100             IN   PTR         myserver.home.test.
100             IN   PTR         mail.home.test.
100                  IN     PTR     www.home.test.
100                  IN     PTR     ftp.home.test.
111                  IN     PTR     virtual1.home.test.
112                  IN     PTR     virtual2.home.test.
```

I suggest you to practice configuring a master DNS server including all information in this exercise based on what you have learned previously in this book.

Configuring a forwarding-only name server

For a forwarding-only name server you'll need to construct in the **/var/named/chroot/etc** directory the **named.conf** file as I have explained previously in this chapter.
Don't forget to create a symbolic link of this file in the **/etc/** directory.

- **cd var/named/chroot/etc**
  touch named.conf

The information you need to add into this file is :

```
options {
        directory "/var/named";
        forward only;
        forwarders {
                192.168.1.111;
                192.168.1.112;
                192.168.1.113;
        };
};
```

- **cd /etc**
  ln -s /var/named/chroot//etc/named.conf named.conf

In this case any computer that searches for your DNS server will be forwarded to search data into the computers with the aforementioned IP address already configured as clients.
If the database in these clients can't provide the necessary answer then the computer that makes the query is led to search the default **/var/named/named.ca** file which holds a default list of root DNS servers for the Internet.

Configuring a slave name server

Based on the example used to configure a master DNS server, if you want to have on your network also a slave name server, then you have to setup another computer for this task an create on it the **named.conf** file in the **/var/named/chroot/etc** directory :

    cd var/named/chroot/etc
    touch named.conf

The information you'll add in this file is :

```
zone "home.test" IN {
        type slave;
        file "slave/home.test";
        masters {
                192.168.1.100;
                        };
};
```

I remind you that you'll need also to create a symbolic link of the **/var/named/chroot/etc/named.conf** file in the **/etc** directory:

    cd /etc
    ln -s /var/named/chroot//etc/named.conf named.conf

The slave server will periodically check with your master DNS server (I supposed that your master DNS server is the one configured earlier) and after reading the data from the master server will create in the **/var/named/slaves** directory the zone file named **slave.home.test**

The graphical BIND configuration tool

The Red Hat® Enterprise Linux® based systems provide a graphical tool to configure DNS.
This tool isn't installed by default in your Linux® distribution.
Once you have installed all necessary packages I have already described you could use **yum** or **Pirut** to install the **system-config-bind** package.

A fast way to do this is to type from a terminal:
yum install system-config-bind.
If you prefer **Pirut** then go to the **Servers** section, be sure the **Server Configuration Tools** box is checked and in this group check the box referring to **system-config-bind**.

Once installed you can activate this tool by simply typing from a terminal **system-config-bind** or go to **System**, choose **Administration**, search **Server Settings** and click on **Domain Name System.**

Practice configuring different DNS server types using this tool and the examples I have provided in this chapter.
I have to remind you that once used this tool, it will override all previous DNS settings you might have done.

Chapter 11. DHCP – Dynamic Host Configuration Protocol

As I have presented in Chapter 5, a client computer could obtain statically or dynamically network information.
In this chapter I'll explain the dynamically way of obtaining network information from a server.

There are two protocols designated for this method of acquiring necessary network information in order for a client computer to gain access to Internet:

DHCP   – used when the client computer obtains network configuration data from a DHCP server on the local network.

BOOTP   – used if the client computer needs to acquire network information from a DHCP server on another network.

A simple declaration like `BOOTPROTO=dhcp` in the **/etc/sysconfig/network-scripts/ifcfg-eth0** file of the client computer simplifies the whole procedure to connect to Internet.

DHCP Server Configuration

If you want to configure a computer to be a DHCP server for your network you'll have to install the **dhcp** RPM package while the **dhclient** RPM package should be installed by default:

yum install dhcp

The DHCP server configuration is based on editing it's configuration file **dhcpd.conf** that has to be created.

After installing the **dhcp** RPM package you'll find a model for this file in **/usr/share/doc/dhcp-[version_number]/dhcpd.conf.sample**, where **[version_number]** is the number of the current version for the **dhcp** RPM package.

From a terminal issue the following command:

cat /usr/share/doc/dhcp-[version_number]/dhcpd.conf.sample > /etc/dhcpd.conf

The new created **/etc/dhcpd.conf** file will look like this:

```
ddns-update-style interim;
ignore client-updates;


subnet 192.168.0.0 netmask 255.255.255.0 {

# --- default gateway
        option routers                  192.168.0.1;
        option subnet-mask              255.255.255.0;
        option nis-domain               "domain.org";
        option domain-name              "domain.org";
        option domain-name-servers      192.168.1.1;
        option time-offset         -18000; # Eastern Standard Time
#     option ntp-servers              192.168.1.1;
#     option netbios-name-servers     192.168.1.1;
# --- Selects point-to-point node (default is hybrid). #Don't
change this unless
# -- you understand Netbios very well
#     option netbios-node-type 2;

        range dynamic-bootp 192.168.0.128 192.168.0.254;
        default-lease-time 21600;
        max-lease-time 43200;
  # we want the nameserver to appear at a fixed address
        host ns {
                next-server marvin.redhat.com;
                hardware ethernet 12:34:56:78:AB:CD;
                fixed-address 207.175.42.254;
        }
}
```

The first two entries in this file establish a general behavior of your DHCP server :

`ddns-update-style interim;` shows how DNS server's database it's updated every time the DNS server renews the DHCP leases.

`ignore client-update;` indicates that client computers are not allowed to change their host names.

The `"subnet"` section of this file establishes certain parameters for a specific subnet within the brackets `{ }`.

You could add as many sections as you like referring to different subnets, each and every one having different specified parameters within brackets `{ }`.

For example, your DHCP server might have the following parameters in it's configuration file:

```
ddns-update-style interim;
ignore client-updates;

subnet 192.168.3.0 netmask 255.255.255.0 {
        option routers                  192.168.3.1;
        option subnet-mask              255.255.255.0;
        option nis-domain               "star.net";
        option domain-name              "star.net";
        option domain-name-servers      192.168.3.2;
          option time-offset    -18000; # Eastern Standard Time
        range dynamic-bootp  192.168.3.99 192.168.3.172;
        default-lease-time 21600;
        max-lease-time 43200;
      }
subnet 192.168.88.0 netmask 255.255.255.0 {
        option routers                  192.168.88.1;
        option subnet-mask              255.255.255.0;
        option domain-name              "nitro.home";
      option domain-name-servers      192.168.88.5;
          option time-offset    -18000; # Eastern Standard Time
        option netbios-name-servers     192.168.1.5;
        option netbios-node-type 2;
          range dynamic-bootp  192.168.88.100 192.168.88.110;
```

```
         default-lease-time 3600;
         max-lease-time 10800;
      }
subnet 192.168.24.0 netmask 255.255.255.0 {
            option routers                    192.168.24.2;
              option subnet-mask              255.255.255.0;
              option domain-name              "sonny.work";
              option domain-name-servers      192.168.24.18;
              option time-offset -18000; # Eastern Standard Time
        host nick {
          hardware ethernet 11:77:C3:9:0B:D2;
          fixed-address 192.168.24.20;
        }
        host dan {
          hardware ethernet 1C:F9:63:1:A9:4B;
          fixed-address 192.168.24.31;
        }
}
```

Regarding this example you can conclude that while any client computer from one of the first two subnets will dynamically acquire it's network parameters from within a pre-established IP range of your DHCP server, the client computers being part of the third subnet will have their network parameters sent by your DHCP server accordingly to their unique Hardware MAC Address (hardware ethernet or Ethernet HWaddr if displayed with the **ifconfig eth0** command).

Based on this, what follows will be a presentation of two configuration methods for a DHCP server and also the interaction between the DHCP server and the DNS server, so we'll have a situation closer to reality.

I'll make use of the exercise from Chapter 9 regarding the configuration of a master DNS server.

a)   DHCP server configuration – dynamic address allocation

This type of configuration will serve you very well in case your network is increasing and it will be pretty difficult to keep up with manually IP address allocation for each new client computer added to your network.

As you remember from the precedent chapter, I've considered a small network for which I've established a domain name (**home.test**) hosted by a computer named **myserver.home.test** and two client computers **virtual1** and **virtual2** recognized as being part of the **home.test** domain.

Having your own domain you'll probably want now that any present or future client computer to have it's IP address dynamically acquired from a DHCP server on your domain.

You'll need to modify first some settings in DNS main configuration file **/etc/named.conf** so it will look like this:

```
options {
  listen-on port 53 { 127.0.0.1; 192.168.1.100; };
  listen-on-v6 port 53 { ::1; };
  directory   "/var/named";
  dump-file   "/var/named/data/cache_dump.db";
  statistics-file "/var/named/data/named_stats.txt";
  memstatistics-file "/var/named/data/named_mem_stats.txt";
        query-source    port 53;
        query-source-v6 port 53;
        allow-query     { localhost; 192.168.1.0/24; };
};
logging {
        channel default_debug {
                file "data/named.run";
                severity dynamic;
        };
};

acl "trusted-subnet" { 192.168.1.0/24; };

zone   "home.test" IN {
        type master;
        file "home.test.zone";
        allow-update { key "rndckey"; };
    notify yes;
};
zone "1.168.192.in-addr.arpa" IN {
        type master;
        file "home.test.rev.zone";
        allow-update { key "rndckey"; };
    notify yes;
};
include "/etc/rndc.key";
```

As you can see in this configuration, the **/etc/named.con**f file was modified by introducing fist a basic security declaration :

```
acl "trusted-subnet" { 192.168.1.0/24; };
```

This setting indicates that the DNS server accept it's database to be updated by the DHCP server as long as it refers only to the **192.168.1.0/24** network (your network in this case) declared to be trusted.
Notice that it's based on ACL settings!

You can also introduce in the "options" section of this file a setting that will allow or not the transfer.
For example, you could have:

```
allow-transfer { none; };
          or
allow-transfer { localhost; };
          or
allow-transfer { localhost; 192.168.1.0/24; };
          or
allow-transfer { 192.168.1.0/24; };
```

Observation
There are many options to secure access to your DNS resources.
*Please consult the manual pages for **named.conf** and **BIND 9 Administrator** **Reference Manual** for details.*

For both zones (forward and reverse) you need to introduce also the allow-update directive so you'll have the DHCP server dynamically updating the DNS records.
As you can see, updates are allowed only if the client and the server exchange the same **rndckey** obtained as I have described in Chapter 9.

There are two more modifications necessary to be done in order to have your DHCP server dynamically updating the DNS records:

1. The DNS server needs write permission for all the zone files. Remember that in the previous chapter the zone files were created under **root** authority so now you need **named** to have authority over the zone file.
    You'll need the zone files in the **/var/named** directory (which are symbolic links to files located in the **/var/named/chroot/var/named**

directory) to have permission set to 644 and of course the owner has to be **named** instead of **root**.

> **cd /var/named**
> **chown -h named.named ***
> **chmod 644 ***
> **ls -l /var/named/chroot/var/named**

Make sure that **named** has authority over all forward and reverse files in this directory and also these files have permission set at least to 644. Eventually use the **chown** and **chmod** commands to do this.

2.   I assume that SELinux and Firewall were disabled for practicing configuring the DNS and DHCP servers. Now that **named** has write permission it has to be able to create files in **$ROOTDIR/var/named** directory.

Use a text editor to make active the directives ENABLE_ZONE_ WRITE=yes and ROOTDIR=/var/named/chroot in the **/etc/sysconfig/named** file.

Observation
Be sure that after the ENABLE_ZONE_WRITE=yes entry you will add on the same line a pound character if you don't want to remove the explicative text referring to this setting, so the respective line will look like this:

```
ENABLE_ZONE_WRITE=yes  # If SELinux is disabled, then allow
named #to write
#                                its zone files and create files in
#its $ROOTDIR/var/named
#                                directory, necessary for DDNS and
#slave zone transfers.
#                                Slave zones should reside in the
#$ROOTDIR/var/named/slaves
#                                directory, in which case you would
#not need to enable zone
#                                writes. If SELinux is enabled, you
#must use only the
#                                'named_write_master_zones'
variable #to enable zone writes.
```

For the DHCP server configuration sequence, assuming that you have created the **/etc/dhcpd.conf** file as explained earlier, open this file with a text editor and modify it to look like this:

```
authoritative;
ddns-update-style interim;
ignore client-updates;
ddns-domainname "home.test";
ddns-rev-domainname "1.168.192.in-addr.arpa";

key rndckey {
        algorithm hmac-md5;
        secret
"1eN1nKilt1bN7lR9COkAEYWWcrN5do0I6D9yff3F8hmJXHPUEf5IeUoaelvefe
eQf8vu+16wEkZ0cADBzA7cqQ==";
}

zone home.test. {
        primary 127.0.0.1;
        key rndckey;
        }

zone 1.168.192.in-addr.arpa. {
        primary 127.0.0.1;
        key rndckey;
        }

subnet 192.168.1.0 netmask 255.255.255.0 {

        option routers                  192.168.1.1;
        option subnet-mask              255.255.255.0;
        option domain-name              "home.test";
        option domain-name-servers      192.168.1.100;
          option time-offset -18000; # Eastern Standard Time

          range dynamic-bootp 192.168.1.111 192.168.1.112;
        default-lease-time 60;
        max-lease-time 60;
}
```

Right on the top of this file, through the `authoritative;` parameter, I have informed the clients that the configuration file is correct and for the given subnet segment the DHCP server is also authoritative.

The `ddns-domainname "home.test";` and `ddns-rev-domainname "1.168.192.in-addr.arpa";` parameters were used to make a FQDN (Fully Qualified Domain Name) for dynamic DNS updates and also declared for the forward and reverse zone as specified in the **/etc/named.conf** file.
These parameters are not passed to clients.

I have introduced the **rndckey** generated in the previous chapter located as you remember in the **/etc/rndc.key** file.

Just copy the content of the **/etc/rndc.key** into the **/etc/dhcpd.conf** file but be careful how you do it considering that there are some differences between the the the way the **rndckey** is written in **/etc/rndc.key** file and the way you have to write it into the **/etc/dhcpd** file.

Notice how the forward and reverse zones were introduced in **/etc/dhcpd.conf** file. The `primary 127.0.0.1` statement indicates the master (primary) DNS server for the zone.

Regarding the way your subnet is declared, things are pretty much self explanatory.
The IP address in `option routers 192.168.1.1;` is the IP that your DHCP server will pass to clients as being Gateway.

The `range dynamic-bootp` specifies in this case only two IP addresses that the DHCP server will offer to any known client on your domain. In my example they will be dynamically assigned like this:

> **virtual1.home.test** will have the assign IP address **192.168.1.111**
> **virtual2.home.test** will have the assign IP address **192.168.1.112**

For the `default-lease-time` and `max-lease-time` directives I have established the same short period of time (60 seconds) only to make an easier live observation of your DHCP server once you'll issue the **dhcpd -d -f** command.

Once you're done editing the **/etc/named.conf** and **/etc/dhcpd.conf** files as shown start the servers issuing the following commands:

> **service named start**   - will start the DNS server
> **dhcpd -d -f**   - will start in foreground the DHCP server

Don't forget to issue the **chkconfig named on** and **chkconfig dhcpd on** commands so the servers will start automatically in case you restart your computer. To check your work you'll have to start your client computers (in this case **virtual1.home.test** and **virtual2.home.test**) after you have done the following modifications for each client:

a) The **/etc/hosts** file for **virtual1** must contain:

```
127.0.0.1         localhost.localdomain      localhost
::1               localhost6.localdomain6    localhost6
192.168.1.111     virtual1.home.test         virtual1
```

The **/etc/hosts** file for **virtual2** must contain:

```
127.0.0.1         localhost.localdomain           localhost
::1               localhost6.localdomain6         localhost6
192.168.1.112     virtual2.home.test              virtual2
```

b) The **/etc/sysconfig/network** file for **virtual1** must show:

```
NETWORKING=yes
NETWORKING_IPV6=no
HOSTNAME=virtual1.home.test
```

The **/etc/sysconfig/network** file for **virtual2** must show:

```
NETWORKING=yes
NETWORKING_IPV6=no
HOSTNAME=virtual2.home.test
```

c) The **/etc/sysconfig/network-scripts/ifcfg-eth0** for **virtual1** contains:

```
DEVICE=eth0
BOOTPROTO=dhcp
HWADDR=00:0C:29:AE:DD:CB
ONBOOT=yes
```

The **/etc/sysconfig/network-scripts/ifcfg-eth0** for **virtual2** contains:

```
DEVICE=eth0
BOOTPROTO=dhcp
HWADDR=11:77:C3:9:0B:D2
ONBOOT=yes
```

Of course your HWADDR options will be different from these used in my example. Once you make sure that the aforementioned files were edited as I have shown for both clients, restart the client computers and notice on your server's terminal the messages displayed when each client computer is acquiring it's IP.
Check on each client computer what the **/etc/resolv.conf** file contains.
It should display something similar to this :

```
search home.test
nameserver 192.168.1.100
```

It might be a possibility that when you start for the first time the DHCP server, even if you have restarted your client computers they will display in their **/etc/resolv.conf** file something like :

```
search localhost
nameserver 192.168.1.1
```

This will indicate that the clients did not acquired the desired IP addresses from the range you have established in the **/etc/dhcpd.conf** file.

If this problem occurs just issue on the client computer that troubles you the following commands:

    dhclient -r
      then
    dhclient

This should solve the problem.
To be sure check again the client's **/etc/dhcpd.conf** file.

Observations
If for this exercise you'll use VMware machines (server-client), you should know that Vmware runs it's own DHCP server so your virtual client computer won't be able to dynamically acquire it's IP from your configured

*virtual DHCP server unless you'll "help" the client to do this by issuing from it's terminal **dhclient -r** and **dhclient** commands.*

*If one of your servers refuses to start returning errors check the **/var/log/messages** files.*
You'll find there all the information you'll need to correct any mistake that might occur in the configuration files.

I remind you that every time you make changes in SOA record the version number has to be incremented (YYYYMMDD01, YYYYMMDD02, YYYYMMDD03, etc), where YYYY = year (2008, 2009, etc); MM =month (01 - 12); DD = day (01 - 31).

b) DHCP server configuration – fixed IP address

This configuration is very comfortable as long as you want to create a DHCP server for your network that offers IP address to a small number of client computers. In this case, using virtual machines (server-client) will work just fine with no trouble for the client to acquire it's IP address from a virtual DHCP server configured this way.

Assuming that everything worked fine with the previous configuration of the DNS server, following almost the same pattern, all you have to do for having this type of DHCP server configured is to edit the **/etc/dhcpd.conf** file as follows:

```
authoritative;
ddns-update-style interim;
ignore client-updates;
subnet 192.168.1.0 netmask 255.255.255.0 {

        option routers                  192.168.1.1;
        option subnet-mask              255.255.255.0;
        option domain-name              "home.test";
        option domain-name-servers      192.168.1.100;
        option time-offset -18000; # Eastern Standard Time

  # we want the nameserver to appear at a fixed address
        host virtual1.home.test {
                hardware ethernet 00:0C:29:AE:DD:CB;
                fixed-address 192.168.1.111;
        }
        host virtual2.home.test {
                hardware ethernet 11:77:C3:9:0B:D2;
                fixed-address 192.168.49.112;
        }
}
```

For this type of configuration you notice that in the "subnet" section I've "connected" using specific parameters, client computer's name with a fixed IP address based on the unique Hardware MAC Address of each client.
In other words, when the DHCP server receives a request from a computer having a hardware address **00:0C:29:AE:DD:CB** and/or **11:77:C3:9:0B:D2** it will assign for each client the specified IP address.

After you're done editing the **/etc/dhcpd.conf** file, restart the server and then restart the clients.
Check the **/etc/resolv.conf** of each client.
Use also **dig** and **host** commands issued from the client to check the DNS server and notice the result.

Chapter 12. Network Information System (NIS)

This service helps maintaining a centralized data base containing user names and passwords for Linux® computers.

The main consideration for using such centralized database is that in a large network with computers running Linux®, in order to have access to different computers, users must have an account on each and every system they want to log into.

Instead of creating accounts for each and every user on each and every computer in that specific network, a system administrator will setup a NIS server connected to that network.

For example, if an user from workstation3 wants to access the computer named workstation22, then workstation22 will search it's **/etc/password** file and if any information regarding that specific account is not found, it will be requested (if instructed to do so) from the NIS server configured for that network.

Same functions are provided by another service called LDAP (Lightweight Directory Access Protocol) but this won't be covered in this book.

NIS server configuration

To configure a NIS server you have to install first the necessary packages. This can be done by typing from a terminal **yum install ypserv** or if you prefer the graphical interface type **pirut**, go to **Servers,** select **Network Server** and here you'll find the **ypserv** package.

Observation
I will use for the following exercise the master DNS server and DHCP server already configured in Chapters 10 and 11.

It will be very helpful in a future chapter where I'll make active both Firewall and SELinux preparing things for a closer real life situation even if all servers were basically configured.
Grouping exercises used in some chapters will give you clear examples to analyze making things easier to be understood.

Exercise

Configure the computer named **myserver** (remember that it is already configured to be a master DNS server for the **home.test** domain and also it's a DHCP server for the computers part of the same aforementioned domain) to be a NIS server for the computer **virtual1**.
Create on the NIS servers the following accounts: **nisclient1** and **nisclient2**. Make sure these accounts DO NOT exist on the computer **virtual1**.
The NIS server will share it's **/home** directory to the NIS computer clients (**virtual1** in this case) via NFS.

There are a few easy steps to prepare the computer named **myserver** to be a NIS server.
I'll remind you to check Firewall and SELinux to be disabled on server and client.

Considering that you have already installed **ypserv** on **myserver.home.test**, next step will be setting the NIS domain name.

- Open a terminal on **myserver** and type the following command:

  ypdomainname home.test

- To make this change permanent you'll have to open with a text editor the **/etc/sysconfig/network** file and add the following entry :

  ```
  NISDOMAIN=home.test
  ```

Based on settings I've done when I configured the master DNS server and regarding the new entry you just operated, the **/etc/sysconfig/network** of the computer named **myserver** should list something similar to this:

```
NETWORKING_IPV6=no
HOSTNAME=myserver
NETWORKING=yes
NISDOMAIN=home.test
```

Observation

You can use also the `ypdomainname, ndsdomainname` *and* `hostname` *commands to check your NIS domain, DNS and the name of your machine. The first two commands should give you a response similar to* `home.test` *and the third one should confirm that the name of your server is* `myserver`.

- Open with a text editor the **/var/yp/Makefile** file and modify the following entries as follow:

```
#Should we merge the passwd file with the shadow
#file ?
#MERGE_PASSWD=true|false
MERGE_PASSWD=false
```

```
#Should we merge the group file with the gshadow
#file ?
#MERGE_GROUP=true|false
MERGE_GROUP=false
```

Notice that in the following entry I have introduced `shadow`:

```
all: passwd shadow group hosts rpc services netid
     protocols mail \
   #netgrp shadow publickey networks ethers
   #bootparams printcap \
   #amd.home auto.master auto.home auto.local
   #passwd.adjunct \
   #timezone locale netmasks
```

Save these settings and proceed to the next step.

- Create the file **securenets** in **/var/yp** directory and edit it by adding the net mask of your network and your network in this order. Considering the IP address of **myserver** beeing 192.168.1.100 then the entry you should add will be:

```
255.255.255.0          192.168.1.0
```

Don't forget to save settings before exit!

Observation
Don't start your NIS server without creating and editing the
/var/yp/securenets file first!
As you can see this file declares that only computers in your network are
allowed to access the NIS server password database.
If the file doesn't exist or it is blank then the NIS server will listen to all networks.

- Create the authentication files for the domain **home.test**. After this is
  done, all non privileged accounts created will be accessible via NIS.
  Type from a terminal of your NIS server the following command:

/usr/lib/yp/ypinit -m

The command will show the following dialog:

```
At this point, we have to construct a list of the hosts which
will run NIS servers.  myserver.home.test is in the list of NIS
server hosts. Please continue to add the names for the other
hosts, one per line. When you are done with the list, type a

       <control D>.
             next host to add:
             next host to add:
        The current list of NIS servers looks like this:

       myserver.home.test
```

- Press Ctrl + D keys ass instructed.

- Add the requested users and establish passwords for them:

useradd nisclient1
passwd nisclient1

useradd nisclient2
passwd nisclient2

- Start the services making sure they will start automatically in case
  you'll restart the computer.

service ypserv start
chkconfig ypserv on

and

service yppasswdd start
chkconfig yppasswdd

IMPORTANT: Any time a new account is added on the NIS server you must update NIS database so the new account will be recognized!
Do this by changing directory into **/var/yp (cd /var/yp)** and then type the command **make** in this directory.

The exercise instructs also to configure the computer named **myserver** to be a NFS server sharing the **/home** directory to the computers (**virtual1**) in your network.

Observation
Yes, according to the exercise in Chapter 10, the computer named **myserver** *was used to be a master DNS for two computers in your network:* **virtual1** *and* **virtual2**.
In this exercise I will configure only computer named **virtual1** *to be a NIS client for* **myserver** *on* **home.test** *domain.*
You could extend the requirements of this exercise configuring also the computer named **virtual2** *to be a NIS client on the same domain.*
For this you'll have to follow the same steps I'll describe as for configuring **virtual1** *as a NIS client.*

- Edit the **/etc/exports** file in **myserver** and make it look like this:

```
/home          *(rw,sync)
```

- Export the **/home** directory of the computer named **myserver** on your network with **read** and **write** rights (as specified in the expression above).
From a terminal type:

exportfs -a

- Start the necessary services to have a functional NFS share:

service nfs start
chkconfig nfs on

- Check if **portmap** service is also running and eventually start this service too:

  service portmap status
  service portmap start
  chkconfig portmap on
           or/and
  service portmap restart

- Check if all necessary services are running on the computer named **myserver.**

Use the following commands to determine if NFS shares properly the **/home** directory and if all necessary services required by NIS are up and running (review Chapter 7 if necessary).

- **showmount -e**

This command must return something similar to this:

```
Export list for myserver: /home *
```

- **rpcinfo -p**

The answer from this command should be similar to this:

```
program   vers   proto   port
100000     2     tcp     111   portmapper
100000     2     udp     111   portmapper
100024     1     udp     792   status
100024     1     tcp     795   status
100004     2     udp     942   ypserv
100004     1     udp     942   ypserv
100004     2     tcp     945   ypserv
100004     1     tcp     945   ypserv
100009     1     udp     958   yppasswdd
100011     1     udp     743   rquotad
100011     2     udp     743   rquotad
100011     1     tcp     746   rquotad
100011     2     tcp     746   rquotad
100003     2     udp    2049   nfs
100003     3     udp    2049   nfs
100003     4     udp    2049   nfs
100021     1     udp   32773   nlockmgr
```

```
100021    3    udp   32773   nlockmgr
100021    4    udp   32773   nlockmgr
100003    2    tcp    2049   nfs
100003    3    tcp    2049   nfs
100003    4    tcp    2049   nfs
100021    1    tcp   45376   nlockmgr
100021    3    tcp   45376   nlockmgr
100021    4    tcp   45376   nlockmgr
100005    1    udp     770   mountd
100005    1    tcp     773   mountd
100005    2    udp     770   mountd
100005    2    tcp     773   mountd
100005    3    udp     770   mountd
100005    3.   tcp     773   mountd
```

Move on **virtual1** computer and configure the automounter to mount the shared **/home** directory.

- Create in **/etc** directory a file named **auto.home**

  touch /etc/auto.home

- Edit it as follows:

```
*    -fstype=nfs,rw,soft,intr,timeo=100  myserver.home.test:/home/&
```

Save settings you've made in this new created file and exit.

- Edit the **/etc/auto.master** file and make it refer to the **/etc/auto.home** by introducing this entry:

```
/home     /etc/auto.home     --timeout 120,nosuid
```

Observations
Notice how I used the mounting option `soft` *with* `timeo=100`*.*
Remember the observation made in Chapter 7 regarding NFS as being "stateless".
It is a good idea to review mounting options for NFS, too.

The option `--timeout` *established to be* `120` *seconds is used here for a fast observation of automounter's behavior.*
In this case the automounter will unmount the shared directory /home after 2 minutes.

After editing the **/etc/auto.master** don't forget to save settings on exit.

- Remember to restart the **autofs** service after editing the aforementioned files and also make sure **portmap** service will start next time when you reboot your client computer:

  service autofs restart
  chkconfig autofs on

  service portmap status
  chkconfig portmap on

Configuring the NIS client

Use the graphical tool provided to setup your NIS client.
Go to **System**, choose **Administration** and then select **Authentication** or from a terminal type **system-config-authentication.**
The result will be as follows:

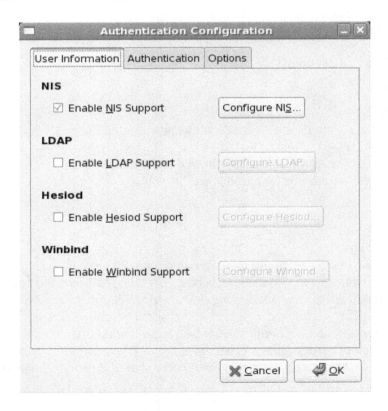

The **User Information** tab provides the necessary information.
Just check the **Enable NIS Support** box to activate **Configure NIS.**

Press the **Configure NIS button** and you'll be prompted to insert the
information regarding the **NIS server** as in the next image:

Fill in the fields regarding **NIS Domain** and **NIS Server** as shown previously
and hit **OK** when done.

This will bring you back to the initial dialog box.
Select the **Options** tab and then check the boxes as shown.

Be sure to check the box **Create home directories on first login**.

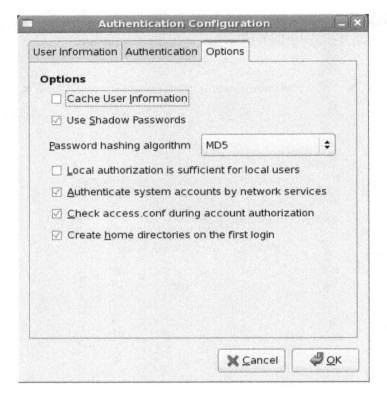

When you're done hit OK and this will restart the **ypbind** service making your client look for the specified NIS server.

The only thing left to be done is making sure everything works as required. For this open a terminal from the NIS server and use **ssh** to login as **nisclient1** or **nisclient2** on the machine named **virtual1.**

     ssh nisclient1@virtual1.home.test

             or

     ssh nisclient2@virtual1.home.test

Both commands will prompt to introduce the necessary password for one of the required NIS users.

If everything was done correctly you'll be able to login as **nisuser1** or **nisuser2.**
You can verify this also from the client machine (**virtual1**) by logging in as one of the aforementioned NIS users.

On the NIS server, **root** can change passwords using the **passwd nisuser** command. On the NIS client computer, **root** should change passwords by typing **yppasswd -p nisuser** while regular users should change their passwords using the **yppasswd** command.

I remind you to check if the **yppasswdd** service is running on the NIS server. While logged in as root on the NIS server you can not (and there's no reason to) change passwords using the **yppasswd** command.

Chapter 13. Securing Access To Services

Beside configuring different services, a system administrator must know how to protect his system making it as secure as possible.
The Red Hat® Enterprise Linux® distributions provide several tools that help enhancing the security of a certain system and network.

A good idea is to keep on your system only services you need so you'll be able to limit access to the respective services and also to have a better control over the incoming or outgoing traffic.

Establish security levels for different users.
For example if an attacker obtains somehow one of your user's access password, by setting a certain security level for users, the attacker won't gain access to important files and services and, what's more important, taking over your system will be difficult.

The tcp_wrappers system

This system is enabled by default and uses two key files: **/etc/hosts.allow** and **/etc/hosts.deny**.

A network request for a service on your system will be passed to the **tcp_wrappers** which will handle it according to the rules established in the aforementioned files.

If a match is found in **hosts.allow** file the access will be granted while for any match found in **hosts.deny** access will be denied.

If both files **hosts.allow** and **hosts.deny** do not specify any access rule then access is granted by default.

The system permits specifying the daemons you want access to be granted or denied for per user, IP address, domain, network.

An example of what could contain the **/etc/hosts.allow** file:

```
ALL : ALL
ALL EXCEPT telnetd : *.mondo.net
ALL : .green.home EXCEPT mike@station3.green.home
sshd,vsftpd : 192.168.1.0/255.255.255.0
```

First line (ALL : ALL) allows access to all computers that might require access to any active service on your system.

Second line (ALL EXCEPT telnetd : *.mondo.net) states that any computer on **mondo.net** domain is allowed to use any active service on your system but not the **telnetd** service.

Third line (ALL : .green.home EXCEPT mike@station3.green.home) declares that the whole **green.home** domain has access granted to any active service on your system except user **mike** on **station3**.

Finally the forth line (sshd,vsftpd : 192.168.1.0/255.255.255.0) grants access to sshd and vsftpd services for computers being part of the 192.168.1.0 network.
Remember that you have to declare the network and the subnet mask this way because the expression 192.168.1.0/24 is not recognized by the tcp_wrappers.

Now judge for yourself what happen if all these entries would be contained in **/etc/hosts.deny** file.

Detailed information is found consulting the man pages (**man hosts.allow**).

Configuring Firewall

Firewall is a system implemented in hardware, software or a combination of both designed to prevent unauthorized Internet users from accessing Intranets.
An active Firewall will analyze any incoming and outgoing message and if the message doesn't meet the specified set of rules it will be blocked.

You can specify a set of rules with the **iptables** command. The **iptables** command refers to the **Ipv4 class** but if you have to establish rules for the **Ipv6 class** then the command will be **ip6tables.**

The general format when using the **iptables** command is :

```
iptables [-t tabletype] [command] [packet_pattern] -j [action]
```

Based on the **iptables** manual (**man iptables**) I'll describe briefly the components forming the "chain" above.

```
[-t tabletype]
```

The `-t` option (or `--table`) specifies what type of table will be used. There are four types of table:

filter   - sets rules for filtering packets using:

      INPUT   - to check all incoming packets against the rules in this chain.

      OUTPUT   - to check all outgoing packets against the rules in this chain.

      FORWARD   - to check all packets sent to another computer against the rules in this chain.

  nat   - configures **NAT** (Network Address Translation) also known as masquerading using:

      PREROUTING - to alter the incoming packets
      POSTROUTING- to alter the outgoing packets
      OUTPUT   - to alter locally-generated packets before routing

  mangle   - configures specialized packet alteration using:

      INPUT   - for packets coming into the box
      OUTPUT   - for altering locally-generated packets before routing

      FORWARD   - for altering packets being routed through the box

PREROUTING - for altering incoming packets before routing

POSTROUTING - for altering the outgoing packets

raw - configures exemptions from connection tracking in combination with the NOTRACK target using:

PREROUTING - for packets arriving via any network interface

OUTPUT - for packets generated by local processes

`[command]`

I'll describe only four basic commands here but you can find more details by accessing **man iptables.**

-A (--append) - appends one or more rules to the end of the chain

-D (--delete) - deletes a rule from the chain

-L (--list) - lists all currently rules

-F (--flush) - flushes all the rules in the current **iptables** chain

When you append to a chain (**-A**) or delete (**-D**) from a chain you'll have to apply the action to incoming data (**INPUT**), outgoing data (**OUTPUT**), or data being sent to another computer (**FORWARD**).

`[packet_pattern]`

Given the complexity of the `[packet_pattern]` (see **man iptables**) I'll refer only to TCP/IP.
I remind you that in TCP/IP packets are transported using TCP, UDP and ICMP protocols.

A simple example would be the use of `-s [ip_address]` switch.
This will check all packets for a specific source IP address.

On the other hand, when using the `-d [ip_address]` switch all packets will be checked for a specific destination IP address.

More than this, by using the right switch, you can specify the protocol type (`-p tcp` or `-p udp` or `-p icmp`) followed by the destination port (`--dport 3128`, `--dport 53`, etc).

`-j [action]`

Finally the last part of the **iptables** command presents the action that has to be taken after **iptables** finds a packet pattern match.

This action could be as follows:

-j ACCEPT	– packet accepted and follows the rules established by **-A** command
-j REJECT	– packet is dropped and an error message (Destination Host Unreachable) is sent to the computer that requested it.
-j DROP	– packet is dropped without any message sent to the requested computer.

A few examples will clarify everything:

1. Define a rule that doesn't allow any traffic from 192.168.111.0 network.

    ```
    iptables -A INPUT -s 192.168.111.0/24 -j DROP
    ```

Observation
*Notice the use of **iptables** command without specifying `-t filter`.*
*This is possible because default is `-t filter` so in this case **iptables** command assumed that I want to modify a filtering rule.*
Also the computer that tries to connect to my machine won't receive any message (see the `-j DROP` definition).

2. Considering that 192.168.1.0/24 is your local network define a rule that rejects ping attempts from any computer outside this network.

    ```
    iptables -A INPUT -s ! 192.168.1.0/24 -p icmp -j REJECT
    ```

Observation
In the expression above notice the exclamation point (!).

*It inverts the meaning saying (referring to this example) "any network is
rejected to use ping EXCEPT computers part of 192.168.1.0/24 network".*

3. Define a rule that allows computers in your network to access the
    proxy server for your LAN. (I assumed that Squid was already
    configured).

```
iptables -A INPUT -p tcp --dport 3128 -j ACCEPT
```

If you want to delete a rule (I'll use the rule defined in the third example) you
have to type :

```
iptables -D INPUT -p tcp --dport 3128 -j ACCEPT
```

After your Firewall rules were defined, remember that for saving them in the
/etc/sysconfig/iptables you'll need to type :

service iptables save

Doing this, in case of restart the established rules won't be lost so your
Firewall will load them at startup.

You can also edit the **/etc/sysconfig/iptables-conf** and set one of the
following options to **yes** (default they're set to **no**) :

```
IPTABLES_SAVE_ON_STOP="yes"
IPTABLES_SAVE_ON_RESTART="yes"
```

The options are self explanatory: first option will save your established rules
when Firewall is stopped while the second will save the rules when Firewall
is restarted.

Red Hat® Enterprise Linux® 5 based distributions give you the possibility to
use a graphical interface when configuring Firewall.

This can be called by typing from a terminal **system-config-securitylevel** (**system-config-securitylevel-tui**) or you can go to **System**, choose **Administration** and then click on **Security Level and Firewall**.

When Firewall is active, by default, in the **Trusted services** section none of the displayed services are set to accept connections.

However Firewall accepts by default the use of **ping** command coming from other computers, access external DNS as also support for Internet Printer Protocol (by typing in your web browser **http://localhost:631**, you should be able to configure a printer attached to your computer or a network printer without configuring additional settings for your computer's Firewall).

If you want Firewall to allow traffic to any of the services displayed there, you'll need to check the box for the specific service.

In case the service you want Firewall to allow traffic for is not displayed you'll need to know the port that service operates through.

For example, if you've configured Squid to be the proxy server for your network and your Firewall is up and running then you'll need to tell Firewall to accept traffic through the default **TCP port 3128** port.

You can do this by clicking on **Other ports** in the menu and add the desired port with the desired protocol.

There are some useful commands you'll want to use in order to determine what services are running on your system and what ports they're using :

netstat -natu
nmap -sTU localhost
rpcinfo -p localhost

Observations
*Be sure that **nmap** service is installed in your computer.*
*Use **Pirut** or **yum** to install **nmap** if the service is not installed already.*
*For example from a terminal type **yum install nmap** or **yum install nmap*** if*
you want a graphical interface for this service.

These commands will help you see what ports are opened on your system and what services are running so you can tell Firewall to accept traffic through some ports and/or deny unwanted services on your system to accept connections from other computers.

Remember that the best way to protect your system is to maintain and configure only the services you need. This way, all you have to do is to tell Firewall to accept traffic only through a limited number of ports.

Network Address Translation (NAT)

NAT is a procedure that allows hiding the IP address of an entire private network behind a single IP address.
That means that if your private network consists in multiple computers, using this procedure you'll need only one IP address to connect your entire private network to Internet.

How is this working?

Review the discussion in Chapter 5 where I used as examples the private network IP address 192.168.1.100 and an the "external" IP address used by a router 77.77.77.100.
Let's say the computer with the IP address 192.168.1.100 requests a web page from the Internet.
This request will be first passed to the router through the Gateway of you LAN which in this case might be 192.168.1.1.

The router will cache the IP address that made the request, then it will replace the 192.168.1.100 IP address and the port number with 77.77.77.100 that is it's IP address and also assigns a new port number.

After this, the request will be passed to the Internet for further queries but it will appear to come from a computer having the IP address 77.77.77.100. When the requested web page is found it will come back through your router and passed to the computer that made the original request.

This procedure is also known as **IP Masquerading** and offers two clear advantages: as the Ipv4 class is running out of options and until Ipv6 class will be ready to take it's place, **IP Masquerading** holds on preventing class from quickly exhausting and also, from the security point of view, it won't be easy for an attacker to brake into your system.

In the following exercise I'll present the steps you must follow in case you'll need to use the **IP Masquerading** procedure.

Exercise

Your private network contains 100 computers and all must have Internet access but you have only one official IP address that is 77.77.77.68. One of your computers has two network cards (eth0 and eth1).This will be your firewall.

Given this situation connect all computers of this LAN to Internet.

I assume that you'll choose for your LAN a range of private IP addresses from 192.168.1.1 to 192.168.1.100 inclusive.

In this case your subnet mask will be 255.255.255.0.

- Supposing that the firewall connects to Internet through **eth1** and to LAN through **eth0**, then for this computer you'll have to edit the **/etc/sysconfig/network-scripts/ifcfg-eth0** file by adding something similar to this:

```
DEVICE=eth0
HWADDR=00:0C:29:5F:78:E7
IPADDR=192.168.1.1
NETMASK=255.255.255.0
GATEWAY=192.168.1.1
ONBOOT=yes
```

Observation
*Obviously, you'll have to configure in a similar way also the **eth1** network card using the parameters (regarding Gateway, Nameserver, Netmask) provided by your ISP along with the 77.77.77.68 IP address.*

- Enable **IP Masquerading** for all your private network (192.168.1.0/24) that uses the **eth1** network card to connect to Internet by typing from a terminal of you firewall :

```
iptables -t nat -A POSTROUTING -s 192.168.1.0/24 -o eth1 -j MASQUERADE
```

- Next step will be enabling **IP forwarding** so your firewall computer will be able to act as a router completing the **IP Masquerading** procedure.
  A fast way to do this is by typing from a terminal:

  echo 1 > /proc/sys/net/ipv4/ip_forward

This will enable IP forwarding right away but when you'll restart your system, value **1** established with the previous command will be replaced with the default value **0** in **/proc/sys/net/ipv4/ip_forward** file.

- In case your system will be rebooted, in order to preserve changes done previously you can either manually edit the **/etc/sysctl.conf** file changing net.ipv4.ip_forward = 0 into net.ipv4.ip_forward = 1 or, you can use the following command:

  sysctl -w net.ipv4.ip_forward=1

Observation
Notice the difference between the expressions presented.
*In /etc/syscl.conf file the entry is net.ipv4.ip_forward = 1 and when using the **syctl** command the expression **sysctl -w net.ipv4.ip_forward=1** doesn't contain any spaces between the parameter and it's value!*

- As for the other computers, you'll need to configure every individual network card by allocating different IP addresses (from 192.168.1.2 to 192.168.1.100) but using the same IP address for Gateway (in this example 192.168.1.1).

Observation

It is not so "elegant" (better said unproductive!) to manually modify one hundred network configuration files introducing network parameters for each and every computer of your LAN.

*A faster way would be configuring your firewall computer to be also a DHCP server (see Chapter 11 the **DHCP Server – dynamic address allocation** section).*

Security Enhanced Linux (SELinux)

SELinux is a feature developed by US National Security Agency implementing the mandatory access control mechanism (MAC) in the Linux® kernel providing another level of security making more difficult for an attacker to gain access to files or services.

Given the complexity of SELinux for a better understanding of how this works I recommend you to consult the documentation provided by Red Hat at **http://www.redhat.com/docs/manuals/enterprise/RHEL-4-Manual/ selinux-guide/** or by Fedora Project at **http://docs.fedoraproject.org/selinux-user-guide/f12/en-US/index.html** as also the documentation provided by US National Security Agency at **http://www.nsa.gov/research/selinux/index.shtml**.

SELinux could have the following statuses: **enforcing, permissive** (this mode doesn't stop anything but will log any violated rule) and **disabled**.

Once activated, SELinux will let you choose two policies for protecting your system: **targeted** or **strict**. My advice is to go with the default one which is **targeted** so you'll have the possibility to customize what you want.

The **getenforce** command will show the current status of SELinux (enforcing, permissive, disable).
A fast way to activate SELinux is by using the **setenforce** command.

> **setenforce enforcing**   - activates SELinux with default targeted policy
> **setenforce permissive** - activates SELinux in permissive mode

You can also activate SELinux by editing the **/etc/sysconfig/selinux** file choosing the status and policy you want but this way settings will be applied next time when the computer is rebooted.

The **/etc/sysconfig/selinux** file contains all necessary explanations as shown in the following example:

```
# This file controls the state of SELinux on the system.
# SELINUX= can take one of these three values:
#       enforcing - SELinux security policy is enforced.
#       permissive - SELinux prints warnings instead of enforcing.
#       disabled - SELinux is fully disabled.
SELINUX=enforcing
# SELINUXTYPE= type of policy in use. Possible values are:
#       targeted - Only targeted network daemons are protected.
#       strict - Full SELinux protection.
SELINUXTYPE=targeted
# SETLOCALDEFS= Check local definition changes
SETLOCALDEFS=0
```

Notice in my example that SELinux is enabled in enforcing mode **SELINUX=enforcing)** with targeted policy (**SELINUXTYPE=targeted**).

Another way to activate SELinux is to type from a terminal **system-config-securitylevel** and then select the tab **SELinux**. In **SELinux Settings** section you'll have the possibility to activate the service in one of the aforementioned modes.

When SELinux is activated devices, directories and files included are defined as objects wile processes are defined as subjects.

Under these circumstances, objects and subjects are labeled with a context (SELinux user, role, type and an optional level) providing additional information when access control decisions will be done.

The contexts are displayed when using the **ls -lZ** command.
For example when I used the **ls -lZ** command for my **/var/www** directory, regarding the **/var/www/html** directory, it displayed the following:

```
drwxrwxrwx   root root  system_u:object_r:httpd_sys_content_t html
```

Notice in this case that the object `html` was labeled by SELinux with the following contexts: SELinux user `system_u`, role `object_r` and type `httpd_sys_content_t`.

Regarding the subjects (remember that SELinux define processes as subjects) the contexts can be displayed with the **ps -eZ | grep [process_name]** command.

For my **sendmail** process the **ps -eZ | grep sendmail** command returned:

```
system_u:system_r:sendmail_t     5640 ? 00:00:00 sendmail
system_u:system_r:sendmail_t     5655 ? 00:00:00 sendmail
```

The settings used by SELinux are boolean type.
This means that assigning the value **1** a certain feature will be turned on and assigning the value **0** the feature will be turned off.

These booleans are stored in **/selinux/booleans** directory.
You can display them with the **ls -l /selinux/booleans** command.
A more useful command that will display the booleans and also showing the status of all of them (on or off) is **getsebool -a.**

Once found the status of the desired boolean with the aforementioned command you can tun it on with **setsebool** command.

For example if you have configured a HTTP server where clients will have access to home directory you'll need to "tell" SELinux that this action is permitted.

This is done by turning on the `httpd_enable_homedirs` boolian in the **/selinux/booleans** directory.

By default the assigned value for `httpd_enable_homedirs` is **0.** Check it with the **getsebool httpd_enable_homedirs** command.
To enable this feature just type from a terminal the following command:

setsebool -P httpd_enable_homedirs 1

The command will change the default value **0** into **1** for the aforementioned feature.

By turning on or off different features in **/selinux/booleans** directory basicly SELinux will allow or deny access to specific files, directories or processes as long as they use their default locations.

For example, regarding the HTTP service, turning on specific booleans will be enough to allow clients login and retrieve files from your Apache Server as long as the default directory (**/var/www/html**) was mentioned to be used in the **/etc/httpd/conf/httpd.conf** file.

But if you have configured a non-standard directory for your HTTP Server, then SELinux will not allow access to this directory and clients won't be able to retrieve files from your server.
Remember that SELinux labels objects and subjects with different contexts. As I've showed you previously the context for the **/var/www/html** directory was:

```
drwxrwxrwx  root root  system_u:object_r:httpd_sys_content_t html
```

Assuming that instead of **/var/www/html** directory you've configured your Apache Server to use a new created directory **/new_html**, the contexts of this directory will be:

```
drwxrwxrwx   root root  root:object_r:default_t  new_html
```

SELinux will allow clients to access this directory ONLY if the contexts will be the same as for the **/var/www/html** directory.

For this to happen you'll need to use the **chcon** command as follows:

chcon -R -u system_u /new_html
chcon -R -t httpd_sys_content_t /new_html

Observations
The command could be used also this way:

> *chcon -R -u system_u -t httpd_sys_content_t /new_html*

The -R switch was used to make sure that not only the contexts of the aforementioned directory are changed but also all included files and/or directories.

Always remember to change contexts of non-standard directories and make them be the same as with the default directory used by the service you have configured.

In case you made a mistake when relabeling your files or directories, use the **restorecon -F [desired_directory]** or **restorecon -R [desired_directory]** commands replacing of course **[desired_directory]** with the path to the directory that needs to be relabeled.

SELinux Management Tool

If you consider that using the command line for changing different settings in SELinux is not comfortable for you, then you have the possibility to use the SELinux Managamet Tool.

To use this graphical tool, make sure you have installed the **policycoreutils-[version_number].rpm** and **policycoreutils-gui-[version_number].rpm** packages where **[version_number]** is the number of the current version for the aforementioned packages.

You can install these packages using Pirut or from a terminal type:

> **yum install policycoreutils***

Once all packages installed and SELinux activated (at least in **permissive** mode) you can start SELinux Management Tool from a terminal by typing **system-config-selinux** or go to **System**, choose **Administration** and then click on **SELinux Management**.

This should bring up the following menu:

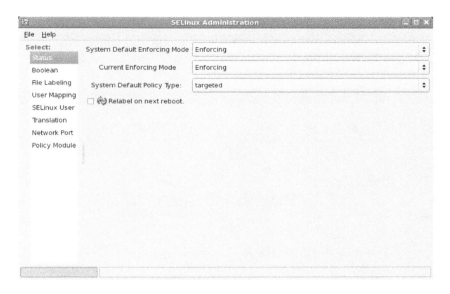

Notice in this menu you have also the possibility to enable or disable SELinux once the **Status** option is highlighted.

To change the settings for booleans highlight the **Boolean** option in the left panel and then check the desired boolean in the right panel.

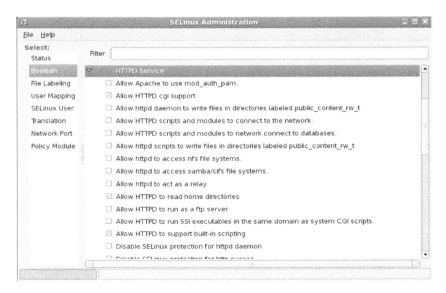

In this example a double click on **HTTPD Service** shows all booleans SELinux controls this service with.

If you want to change the default labels for files and directories you'll have to click on **File Labeling.**

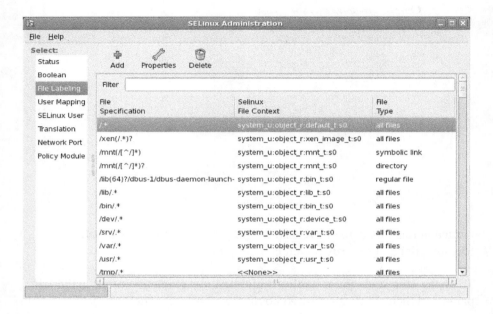

The menu offers you the possibility to see the default labels for different files, to modify them and even to add new files or directories for which you want to apply the desired label.
Modifying settings here is the equivalent of using the **chcon** command described earlier.

I'll remind you the previous example with the non-standard **/new_html** directory for your HTTP Server and show how to apply the aforementioned label **(httpd_sys_content_t)** for it but this time using the SELinux Management Tool.

Click on the **Add** button and the following menu will appear:

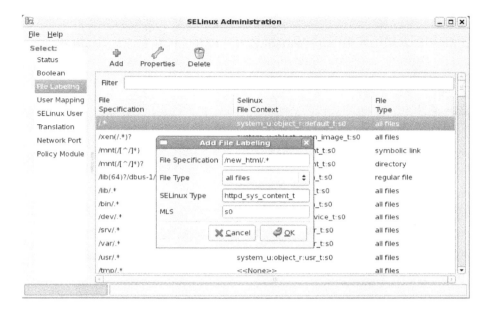

Notice how the **/new_html** directory is labeled so SELinux will allow access to this directory for the clients of your HTTP Server.
When you're done with these settings just press OK and you're label is applied.

Labeling problems might occur sometimes so apparently one solution to solve these problems is consulting the log files located in **/var/log/audit/audit.log.** This would be a very difficult task considering the volume of information displayed there.

Fortunately SELinux comes with a graphical tool – **Setroubleshoot Browser** - that helps you detect the problem and even advising you with commands that should be used in case your system encounters labeling problems.

Check the existence of the following packages by using the **rpm -qa | grep setroubleshoot** command.
The command should return something similar to this:

> **setroubleshoot-[version_number]**
> **setroubleshoot-plugins-[version_number]**
> **setroubleshoot-server-[version_number]**

If the packages are not installed use **Pirut** or, from a terminal type :

   yum install setroubleshoot*

You can initiate the **Setroubleshoot Browser** by going to **Applications**, choose **System Tools** and then click on **SELinux Troubleshoot** or by issuing from a terminal the **sealert -b** command.

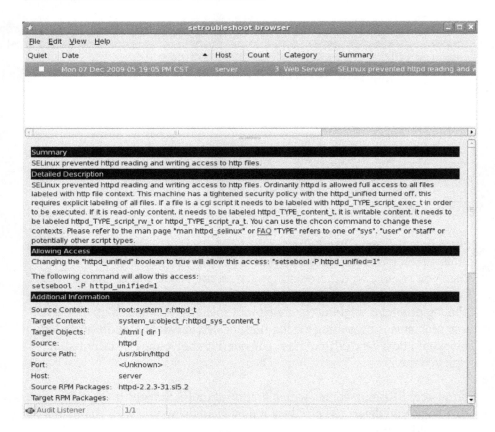

Observations
If you add another disk to your machine that wasn't labeled via SELinux you might receive alerts indicating serious labeling problems.
*To solve this problem use the **restorecon -R -v [device]** command.*

*Same thing might happen if you have created files when SELinux was disabled. In this case the **touch /.autorelabel** and then **reboot** commands should solve the problem.*

Chapter 14. Using Firewall and SELinux

Along this book you have configured different servers but I've always recommended to disable Firewall and SELinux.
Time has come now to enable both services.

A fast way to enable both services is to type from a terminal :

system-config-securitylevel

In the initiated menu enable Firewall and then make sure to activate SELinux in **enforcing** mode.

I'll remind you to check and eventually install all necessary packages for SELinux as I've explained in the previous chapter.

What follows presents some minimal settings for Firewall and SELinux regarding the servers you have configured in previous chapters of this book.

The Web Server

a) Firewall
Depending what type of server you have configured (HTTP or HTTPS) by checking the corresponding options in **Security Level Configuration** tool, **WWW (HTTP)** or **Secure WWW (HTTPS)** the clients will have access granted to the corresponding service.
That means Firewall will accept connections through **TCP port 80** and/or **TCP port 443.**
I remind you that the use of **iptables** command will do the same but in this case for the settings to remain active after rebooting your computer it is

necessary to edit and modify the following features in
/etc/sysconfig/iptables-config file:

```
IPTABLES_SAVE_ON_STOP="yes"
IPTABLES_SAVE_ON_RESTART="yes"
```

Assuming that you want to use the **iptables** command then, for adding **TCP port 80** and **TCP port 443** type the following:

> **iptables -A INPUT -p tcp --dport 80 -j ACCEPT**
> **iptables -A INPUT -p tcp --dport 443 -j ACCEPT**

In Chapter 6 I've mentioned Squid Server as part of the Web Server package. It's appropriate to say that you'll need **TCP port 3128** opened in Firewall. Add this port using the **Security Level Configuration** tool or the **iptables** command:

> **iptables -A INPUT -p tcp --dport 3128 -j ACCEPT**

For security reasons you might want to redirect all traffic through **TCP port 80** to **TCP port 3128.**
This is done by adding a new Firewall rule like this:

> **iptables -t nat -A PREROUTING -i eth0 -p tcp --dport 80 -j REDIRECT   --to-ports 3128**

The command will take all traffic from network card eth0 (**-i** switch) through **TCP port 80** and forward it to **TCP port 3128.**
Note that this action is possible only by using the **iptables** command.

b) SELinux
Referring to the HTTP (HTTPS) server in Chapter 6 use the **SELinux Administration** tool to enable the necessary booleans according to requirements of the exercises presented there.

If you have changed the `DocumentRoot` as shown in the exercise into `DocumentRoot "/home/mike/public"` you must "tell" SELinux that clients are allowed to connect to the **public** directory located in mike's home directory. This means the boolean **httpd_enable_homedirs** should be turned on.
Use the SELinux administration tool or simply the following command:

> **setsebool -P httpd_enable_homedirs 1**

Don't forget to label any non-standard directory you might use for your HTTP (HTTPS) server.

According to the requirements of the exercise referring to Virtual Hosts in Chapter 6 verify and eventually change labels for the **/var/www/html/number_one** and **/var/www/html/number_two** directories.

This means that **number_one** and **number_two** directories must have the same label as **/var/www/html** directory.

The **ls -lZ** command should return for **/var/www/html** directory something like this:

```
drwxrwxrwx root root system_u:object_r:httpd_sys_content_t html
```

You can use the **chcon** command to change the labels of the aforementioned directories and make them be the same as for the **/var/www/html** directory:

chcon -R -u system_u -t httpd_sys_content_t /var/www/html/number_one
chcon -R -u system_u -t httpd_sys_content_t /var/www/html/number_two

When you have configured secure Virtual Hosts remember that in the root directory you have created the directory named **secure_web.**

You have to assign also for this directory and for all it's content the same label mentioned before:

chcon -R -u system_u -t httpd_sys_content_t /secure_web

Referring to Squid proxy server all you have to do is to activate the **squid_connect_any** boolean.

Use the graphical tool or faster, use the following command:

setsebool -P squid_connect_any 1

The Network File System (NFS) Service

a) Firewall

Using the **Security Level Configuration tool** and checking the NFS4 box is not enough to share files via NFS. This will activate only the **TCP** and **UDP port 2049** used by NFS but remember that this service needs **portmap**, **mountd** and **rquotad** daemons running to insure access to shared directories on your NFS server.

Again, I remind you to use the **nmap -sTU localhost** and **rpcinfo -p localhost** commands so you'll see all open ports on your computer.

The **rpcinfo -p localhost** command will be very useful in this case because it helps you find the ports used by **portmap** (**TCP** and **UDP port 111**).
As for the **mountd** and **rquotad** daemons the **/etc/sysconfig/nfs** file includes the following entries:

```
MOUNTD_PORT=892 and RQUOTAD_PORT=875.
```

Activate these entries to establish the respective ports for the aforementioned daemons.
In the end you'll need to tell Firewall to accept traffic through the following ports: **TCP/UDP port 111, TCP/UDP port 875, TCP/UDP port 892** and of course the already added **TCP/UDP port 2049** once NFS4 box was checked.

b) SELinux
The NFS server created in Chapter 7 was sharing via NFS the **/home/mike/public** directory.
Remember that the aforementioned directory was shared read-only so for this situation the client computers will be able to mount the shared directory on your server only if you'll turn on the **nfs_export_all_ro** feature.
If you're in a hurry use the following command:

> **setsebool -P nfs_export_all_ro 1**

I'll remind you to change context of any new created directory if you want it shared properly via NFS.

> **chcon -R -u system_u /[shared_directory]**

The File Transfer Protocol service (vsftp)

a) Firewall
The **nmap -sTU localhost** command will display **TCP port 21** allocated for the FTP service.
Use the **Security Level Configuration** tool to check the correspounding box FTP or the **iptables** commnad :

> **iptables -A INPUT -d tcp --dport 21 -j ACCEPT**

b)SELinux

The exercise in Chapter 7 send users mike, nick and john to "jail" into their own home directories when they login via FTP.

This action is permitted by SELinux if you'll turn **ftp_home_dir** on.

setsebool -P ftp_home_dir 1

When using the SELinux Administration tool the equivalent of the command above will be checking the box correspounding to **Allow ftp to read/write files in the user home directories.**

The Samba Services

a) Firewall

In Security Level Configuration check the box correspounding to **Samba.** This action will open**TCP port 139** and **445** as also **UDP port 137** and **138** so your Firewall will allow the designated client computers for your Samba server to have access to files and printers shared via Samba.

b) SELinux

When editing the **/etc/samba/smb.conf** file, you'll find there in the **SELINUX NOTES** section indications on what booleans you have to set on and how to use the **chcon** command to set the appropriate label for the directories you've created and designated to be shared via Samba.

Use the SELinux Administration tool or **setsebool** command to obtain the desired settings for your server.

Sendmail and Dovecot

a)Firewall

The SMTP service works through **TCP port 25** while **POP3** and **IMAP** uses **TCP port 110** respectively **TCP port 143** for communication.

If you check the box corresponding to **Mail (SMTP)** while using the graphical configuration tool, then connections coming through **TCP port 25** will be allowed.

In case your Mail server uses POP3 and/or IMAP then you'll have to add the aforementioned TCP ports corresponding to these services.

In Chapter 8 is presented an example where I used secure versions for SMTP, POP3 and ICMP.
Using the **nmap -sTU localhost** command you'll discover that for a secure mail server (admitting that Dovecot was configured with both secure versions POP3S and ICMPS), Firewall needs to allow connections through the following ports: **TCP port 465** (SMTPS), **TCP port 995** (POP3S) and **TCP port 993** (IMAPS).

Add these ports using the graphical configuration tool for Firewall or the **iptables** command.
If **spamassassin** is used, then you'll have to tell Firewall to allow connections also from the **TCP port 783.**

b) SELinux
Regarding the examples presented in Chapter 8 there are no additional settings to turn on or off for SELinux to handle Sendmail and Dovecot. Even if you use **spamassassin** the default booleans will allow your Mail server to accept incoming mail from your LAN or computers from outside your network.

SSH and NTP

a) Firewall
Once enabled the box correspounding to **SSH** in Security Level Configuration this will determine Firewall to allow traffic through **TCP port 22** for your SSH server.

The **NTP** server needs **UDP port 123** to function through Firewall so you'll need to add this port with the graphical tool or with the **iptables** command:

        iptables -A INPUT -p udp --dport 123 -j ACCEPT

b) SELinux
Referring to the examples in Chapter 9 there are no additional settings to be done for SELinux regarding SSH and NTP.

DNS and DHCP

I assumed that following the exercises presented in Chapters 10 and 11 you have configured a master DNS server for you LAN and also a DHCP server operating inside of this domain so any computer in your network will be a client for the configured DHCP server.

a) Firewall

The DNS server works through **TCP/UDP port 53.**
The port is specified in the **named.conf** file but a better view is offered with the **nmap -sTU localhost** command.
You'll need to open these ports in Firewall as also the **TCP port 953** (rndc).

As for the DHCP server, make sure that Firewall allows traffic through **UDP port 67** (dhcps) and **UDP port 68** (dhcpc).

b) SELinux

In the example used in Chaper 11 I've changed the owner and permissions for all files located in **/var/named** directory so **named** could write the zone files.

Once SELinux enabled you need to change back the owner of those files. The following commands will help you reverse the changes done in that example:

> **cd /var/named**
> **chown -h root.named ***

Remember that also the **/etc/sysconfig/named** file was modified.
You'll need to edit this file again but this time suspend the entry
ENABLE_ZONE_WRITE=yes by inserting the pound character (#) in front of it.
After all modifications were done, turn on the **named_write_master_zones** boolean:

> **setsebool -P named_write_master_zones 1**

NIS server

a) Firewall

According to the requirements of the exercise presented in Chapter 12 the NIS server shares via NFS it's **/home** directory, so first make sure Firewall allows NFS traffic through all necessary ports described earlier in this chapter.

Next step will be configuring Firewall to allow traffic through the ports **ypserv** and **yppasswdd** are working through.

If you'll use the **rpcinfo -p localhost** command you'll see the TCP and UDP ports used by the aforementioned services.

Don't add yet in Firewall the displayed ports!

Restart both services (**service ypserv restart** and **service yppasswdd restart**) and issue again the **rpcinfo -p localhost** command.
The command will show this time different values for the same ports!
Any time you'll restart these services the **rpcinfo -p localhost** command will display different values for the TCP and UDP ports.

What's to be done?

For example the **rpcinfo -p localhost | grep ypserv** command displayed the following for my computer:

```
100004 2      udp    859    ypserv
100004 1      udp    859    ypserv
100004 2      tcp    859    ypserv
100004 1      tcp    859    ypserv
```

While the **rpcinfo -p localhost | grep yppasswdd** command displayed:

```
100009 1      udp    736    yppasswdd
```

In this case I've edited the **/etc/sysconfig/network** file and added the following entry:

```
YPSERV_ARGS="--port 859"
```

And then I've edited the **/etc/sysconfig/yppasswdd** file and modified the entry YPPASSWDD_ARGS= like this:

```
YPPASSWDD_ARGS="--port 736"
```

After saving these settings I've added in Firewall the following ports:
TCP port 859, **UPD port 859** and **UDP port 736**

When the services were restarted (**ypserv** and **yppasswdd**) this time the added ports remained unchanged, fact reflected by the use of the **rpcinfo -p localhost** command.

Observation

The port numbers used here were just examples.
*You'll need to use the **rpcinfo** command as I've explained and determine the specific port numbers used by the **ypserv** and **yppasswdd** services on your machine.*

b) SELinux

As long as the NIS server needs the **/home** directory of the server to be exported **read-write** via NFS you may want to turn on the **nfs_export_all_rw** boolean.

    setsebool -P nfs_export_all_rw 1